Y0-BRR-005

kylie kwong
heart&soul

Kylie Kwong was born into a fourth-generation Australian–Chinese family, in Sydney, Australia. She learnt the fundamentals of Cantonese cooking at her mother's side, and went on to develop her strong artistic style by working as a graphic designer and cooking at home, before stepping into the food world full-time. Kylie then honed her skills with several of Australia's most respected chefs, including Neil Perry and Steve Manfredi, and worked at some of Sydney's finest restaurants – Rockpool, Wockpool and Restaurant Manfredi.

At billy kwong, in Sydney's Surry Hills, Kylie has realised her dream of pouring her heart and soul into her own restaurant. And it is a resounding success story, constantly bursting at the seams with hungry diners.

After a successful career in the film business, **Ian Wallace** returned to his first love, photography. His distinctive use of natural light has led Ian to shoot many cookbooks, and to work for some of the world's best food magazines. He is a regular contributor to *delicious.*, *Vogue Entertaining and Travel* and *Inside Out*, among others.

Simon Griffiths is a leading photographer of food, gardens and interiors. His work has appeared regularly in magazines such as *Australian Gourmet Traveller*, *Vogue Living* and *House and Garden*. He has also been the photographer for numerous books, including *Cooking & Travelling in South-West France*, *Salute!* and *Walking the Dog in Italy*.

kylie kwong
heart&soul

photography by **Ian Wallace** and **Simon Griffiths**

LANTERN
an imprint of
PENGUIN BOOKS

ABC
Books

Flagstaff Public Library
Flagstaff, Arizona

Contents

641.5
K98h

Introduction

From memory, it must have been late September or early October 2002 when I received a phone call from a charmingly spoken Englishman called John Godfrey, wanting to know if I was even vaguely interested in meeting him to discuss an upcoming ABC television cooking series. At the time, I was in the middle of doing 150 different things and, quite frankly, was already feeling far too busy for my liking. But, as always, my undying curiosity and passion for new challenges took over . . . and I heard myself agreeing to an initial meeting.

Several months later, it all seems like a blur and I find myself in a completely new and exciting phase of my life. In a philosophical sense, this whole experience is about energy and movement, change and opportunity. I love this essential nature of life, so I have chosen to go with the flow. I want to learn as much as I can from this experience – life is about receiving the gifts from experience, noticing how you react to certain situations you place yourself in, and learning what makes you tick.

While we're filming, I'm also writing this book to accompany the TV series. Although this has taken up a lot of time as well, I've really enjoyed developing and writing these recipes. I'm always thinking of the whole experience when I am creating a dish: what ingredients are in season; what do I love to eat the most; will the individual components of the dish, with their individual personalities, complement one another; how will the textures feel inside the mouth; will the dish look appetising, fresh and vibrant; will the layered and delicious sensations make the tastebuds come alive?

The array of fresh produce that Australia has on offer continues to inspire and motivate me. The following recipes are a celebration of these delicious treats and are a reflection of all the other types of cuisines I love to draw from, the flavours I love experimenting with, the food I enjoy sharing with my friends and family.

I created most of these recipes over the Christmas and New Year holidays, when I had lots of energy, time and space to devote to them. And maybe because it was summertime in Sydney, or maybe just because I was feeling extravagant, I found myself using lots of lobster, Wagyu beef, beautiful organic chickens and all kinds of gorgeous things. I cook with these ingredients because I love them, but please don't feel intimidated: the most important thing is that

soft tones; dusty beautiful pink,
my favourite mushroom hues...

INTUITION

the power of the
mind by which it
immediately perceives
the truth of things
without reasoning or
analysis : a truth
so perceived, immediate
knowledge. In contrast
with immediate...

OFF-
CENTRE &
BLUE...

@mélancholique...

✶ intuitif...

SENSE:

faculty of receiving sensation.
general or particular :
immediate consciousness.
inward feeling. impression.
opinion. mental attitude.
discernment. understanding.
appreciation. faculty for
what is appropriate.
discernible feeling for things
of some particular kind.
one's right wits. soundness
of judgement. reasonableness.
sensible or reasonable
discourse

The
Unbearable
Lightness
of
Being

you seek out the best that's available to you. Ask your butcher what's good – ask for the freshest lamb shanks, the finest beef fillet, the best free-range chickens and ducks – and you'll eat well. Of course, we Chinese could just eat lobster for breakfast, lunch and dinner, but again it's not essential in any of these recipes. You can easily substitute fresh prawns, crabmeat, or even a beautiful fillet of fish. As long as you use the freshest and best ingredients you can find, you can't go wrong.

Some of the recipes are complex, with lengthy ingredient lists and involved techniques. I adore cooking such recipes when I'm relaxed and have plenty of time. They require that you become completely absorbed – lost in the art and pleasure of cooking – and the result is truly gratifying. Many more of the recipes are very simple, and it is these ones that rely solely on the quality of the ingredients. If you have some Tasmanian scallops so pristine you almost can't bear to touch them, or a prime fillet of Wagyu beef that cost a small fortune, then the simplest recipes are the ones to go for!

I guess one of the things I want to achieve at my restaurant, through my books, and now in this TV series is to raise awareness of authentic Chinese cooking: to show that it's not all about lurid sweet and sour pork, MSG-laden sizzling beef, and chicken and cashew nuts in a gloopy sauce. I want to show you the intricacies and delicacy of real Chinese cuisine, and to show how these same skills and techniques can be applied to Western cookery.

So, although my roots are in the Chinese culinary tradition, many of the recipes in this book are based on European and North African cuisine; only a handful are truly Asian in their inspiration. What I found interesting as I was creating and testing these recipes and then making them over and over again in the studio is that, even though they're mostly Western-style dishes, I actually cook a lot of them in a very Asian fashion. No matter what cuisine I'm cooking, I always strive for a balance of sweet, sour, salty and hot flavours. It's all about following your instincts, keeping in mind harmony between flavours, textures and ingredients – Yin and Yang.

This book is divided into eight chapters, which loosely reflect the episodes in the TV series. The chapters are arranged around themes that have influenced me, and which I continue to find relevant and meaningful. These are the things that inspire me, filling my life with substance, enduring memories, warmth and understanding.

Traditional and Contemporary

When I embarked on my journey into the world of television, I resolved to keep a diary of my thoughts and feelings: all about the excitement, the nerves, the fear, the energy of the experience, the adjustment and reorganisation; about allowing my restaurant, billy kwong, to flow onto a different, new and restructured path . . . and also about lying in my bed at night and thinking, 'Oh my goodness, can I do this, why I am I doing this, where will this take me?'

Speaking with director Simon Target, and the executive producer of ABC Television, Richard Reisz, I was delighted and inspired by their vision of this series – it was to have a strong multicultural aspect, with particular reference to life as an Australian-born Chinese person. This really appealed to me. The combination of 'multi' and 'culture' brings to mind beautiful, blended images of large, close-knit families, delicious food and markets, exotic religion and ritual, different skin colours and tones, intriguing customs and traditions, textures and layers within the world of art, literature, drama and music; a richness and a diversity of people and life.

There is a wonderful positivity in the team of people working on this TV series – each time we meet to brainstorm a concept or an episode, we're all left feeling delightfully exhausted and yet exploding with energy. Simon sits in his director's chair and constantly throws things at me: 'Come on, Kyles, what dishes shall we cook for this ep?' 'More, more, I need more,' he says. 'OK, Kyles, let's try and think back to your childhood. What are your fondest memories – who were your friends, what did your mother cook, what was it like?' 'And tell me, Kyles, if you could have your dream kitchen and dining room, what would it be like? Now tell me, Kyles, what was it like growing up as an Australian-born Chinese girl in the suburbs of Sydney? When did you begin your cooking career? Tell me about your great-grandfather and his four wives. Hang on, Kyles, which generation Kwong were you from?' *Phew!*

mrs jang's home-style fried eggs

Serve as a starter for 4,
or as a meal for 2 with steamed rice

1½ cups vegetable oil

4 large free-range eggs

1 tablespoon oyster sauce

small pinch ground white pepper

2 spring onions (scallions), finely sliced

1–2 red bird's eye chillies, finely sliced

This unassuming recipe is actually rather famous now. Everyone who's tried these eggs – whether in the restaurant or at home – just raves about them. They're also a very nostalgic dish for me, because Mrs Jang was my Uncle Jimmy's mother, and she used to cook these eggs for my brothers and me after we'd been working in his noodle factory. They're so simple, fresh and tasty. Where Westerners have fried eggs and bacon, Chinese people have fried eggs with chilli, oyster sauce and spring onions . . .

Heat oil in a hot wok until the surface seems to shimmer slightly. Crack the eggs into a small bowl, then pour into the hot oil. After 2 minutes, reduce heat to allow the bottom of the eggs to become firm and crisp; the yolks should still be runny at this point.

Carefully slide a fish slice under the eggs, lift out of wok and pour off oil. Return eggs to wok and place back over the heat for another 1–2 minutes to crisp further.

Gently remove eggs from wok and drain off any excess oil before easing onto a plate. Drizzle eggs with oyster sauce and garnish with pepper, spring onions and chillies.

sweet and sour pork

This is my version of an old Cantonese classic, which unfortunately tends to be ill-served by some Chinese restaurants. Many people's experience of sweet and sour pork is of chunks of meat that have been dunked in a thick, heavy batter, over-fried in dirty oil, then doused in an MSG-laden sauce made from tomato sauce, tinned pineapple, cornflour and perhaps a few vegetables. My version uses fresh ingredients, and that makes all the difference. Just make sure you start the day before, as the pork needs to marinate overnight.

Cut pork fillets in half lengthways and then into bite-sized pieces on the diagonal. Blend cornflour with water in a medium-sized bowl until dissolved. Add pork, egg yolks, soy sauce, sesame oil and salt, and mix well. Cover and refrigerate overnight.

Peel pineapple and remove the core. Finely slice into pieces. Cut pickled vegetables into julienne and set aside, together with pineapple. Place vinegar, wine, sugar and extra salt in a small pan and stir over low heat until sugar dissolves. Bring to the boil, add garlic and ginger, reduce heat and simmer, uncovered, for 10 minutes. Add pineapple, pickled vegetables, tomato and capsicum, and simmer for a further 10 minutes, or until tomato has broken down slightly and the flavours are balanced. Remove sauce from stove and set aside.

Combine plain flour and extra cornflour. Add to the marinated pork and mix well. Heat vegetable oil in a hot wok until the surface seems to shimmer slightly. Deep-fry pork in batches over high heat for 1 minute, then reduce heat to medium and fry for another 2 minutes, or until pork is almost cooked through. Remove from wok, using a slotted spoon, and drain on kitchen paper.

Gently reheat the sweet and sour sauce. Finally, return all the pork to the hot oil and deep-fry for a further 3 minutes, or until lightly browned, crispy and cooked through. Remove pork from wok and drain well on kitchen paper.

Arrange pork on a platter and sprinkle with Sichuan pepper and salt. Garnish with cucumber and serve immediately with a bowl of the warm sweet and sour sauce.

Serve as part of a banquet for 4

2 × 300 g (10 oz) pork neck fillets

1½ tablespoons cornflour (cornstarch)

1 tablespoon cold water

2 egg yolks, lightly beaten

3 teaspoons light soy sauce

2 teaspoons sesame oil

1 teaspoon sea salt

750 g (1½ lb) ripe pineapple – about half a small pineapple

150 g (5 oz) 'goong goong's pickles' (page 189)

¾ cup rice wine vinegar

5 tablespoons shao hsing wine

½ cup white sugar

1 teaspoon sea salt, extra

4 garlic cloves, crushed

2 tablespoons ginger julienne

1 small ox-heart (beef) tomato, finely sliced

½ cup yellow capsicum (bell pepper) julienne

¼ cup plain (all-purpose) flour

¼ cup cornflour (cornstarch), extra

vegetable oil for deep-frying

pinch Sichuan pepper and salt (page 194)

1 small cucumber, cut into julienne

sizzling beef

Anyone who's been to a Chinese restaurant in Australia knows there's always a dish on the menu called sizzling beef. It's generally surrounded by a heavy, thick sauce or marinade, which I find way too rich, and has a cardboardy, unnatural flavour. I've got no idea why people order it – maybe they get drawn in by the drama of it all, as the hissing and smoking black cast-iron platter weaves its way to their table. Well, my sizzling beef is a much more refined version, where the natural flavour of the meat really shines, lifted by some Sichuan pepper and salt and fresh lemon juice.

Place wine, BBQ sauce, peanut oil, sugar and half the soy sauce and sesame oil in a large bowl. Add beef and, using your hands, mix thoroughly. Cover and refrigerate for 2 hours.

Cut onions in half, then place cut-side down on a chopping board and cut into 2 cm (1 in) wedges. Pull the wedges apart to separate the layers.

Heat extra peanut oil in a hot wok until the surface seems to shimmer slightly. Add onion, ginger and garlic and stir-fry for 1 minute. Add beef to wok, along with its marinade, and sear on one side for about 1 minute, or until lightly browned; do not stir-fry. Turn beef over and sear the other side for a further minute. Add extra wine, kecap manis, 1 tablespoon of soy sauce and extra sesame oil and stir-fry for 1 minute, or until the beef is just tender and the flavours are balanced.

Arrange beef on a platter, sprinkle with remaining soy sauce and Sichuan pepper and salt. Serve immediately with a small bowl of lemon juice on the side.

Serve as part of a banquet for 4

2 tablespoons shao hsing wine

2 tablespoons Chinese BBQ sauce – ideally Leung Cheung Woo brand

1 tablespoon peanut oil

1 teaspoon white sugar

1 tablespoon mushroom soy sauce

¼ teaspoon sesame oil

400 g (13 oz) top-quality beef fillet, cut into 1.5 cm (¾ in) thick slices

2 small white onions, peeled

2 tablespoons peanut oil, extra

6 cm (2½ in) knob ginger, very finely sliced

4 garlic cloves, crushed

1 tablespoon shao hsing wine, extra

1 teaspoon kecap manis

1½ tablespoons mushroom soy sauce, extra

¼ teaspoon sesame oil, extra

pinch Sichuan pepper and salt (page 194)

¼ cup lemon juice

stir-fried thin egg noodles with red onion and bean sprouts

Serve as part of a banquet for 4

My adorable Uncle Jimmy makes *the* best egg noodles. He is committed to quality and freshness, and always uses fresh eggs as opposed to yellow food colouring. The combination of ingredients in the following recipe is simple, yet traditional – the smoky flavour imparted by the vigorous stir-frying is delicious.

¼ bunch choy sum

300 g (10 oz) fresh thin egg noodles

¼ cup peanut oil

1 tablespoon ginger julienne

3 garlic cloves, diced

1 small red onion, cut in half and then into wedges

1 tablespoon sea salt

3 'braised dried chinese mushrooms' (page 186), finely sliced

4 spring onions (scallions), trimmed and cut into 10 cm (4 in) lengths

1 large red chilli, finely sliced on the diagonal

1 teaspoon sesame oil

1 cup bean sprouts

1 tablespoon light soy sauce

pinch Sichuan pepper and salt (page 194)

Trim ends from choy sum, then cut crossways into thirds, wash thoroughly and drain.

Blanch noodles in boiling salted water until 'al dente' – about 2 minutes – and drain immediately. Refresh in cold water, then drain again thoroughly.

Heat oil in a hot wok until the surface seems to shimmer slightly. Add ginger, garlic, red onion and sea salt, and stir-fry for 1 minute, or until fragrant. Add mushrooms and spring onions and stir-fry for 1 minute. Add noodles, choy sum, chilli and sesame oil and stir-fry for a further minute, or until noodles are heated through. Finally, add bean sprouts and soy sauce and stir-fry for 30 seconds.

Arrange noodles in a bowl, sprinkle with Sichuan pepper and salt and serve immediately.

stir-fried pipis with chilli, ginger and spring onions

The Chinese are just mad about seafood, especially all types of shellfish. I particularly like the chewy yet tender character of pipis, and I also love the way pipis, like mussels, drink up and absorb whatever delicious flavours they are combined with. Clams can also be used in this recipe.

Fill a large bowl or bucket with cold water. Add pipis and stand for at least 2 hours, to purge them of any sand. Rinse thoroughly and drain well.

Place 2 cups of water in a wok and bring to the boil. Add pipis and simmer, covered, for about 2 minutes, or until they begin to open. Immediately remove them from the wok, one by one, using tongs. Take care not to overcook the pipis at this stage; you only need to open them. Drain water from wok and dry with kitchen paper.

Pour peanut oil into wok and heat until the surface seems to shimmer slightly. Add ginger, garlic, chillies and onion and stir-fry for 3 minutes, or until onion is lightly browned. Return pipis to wok, along with wine, vinegar, oyster sauce, soy sauce, sugar, spring onions and sesame oil. Stir-fry over high heat for about 2 minutes, or until the sauce is balanced in flavour and coating all the pipis. Transfer to a large bowl and serve immediately.

Serve as part of a banquet for 4

1 kg (2 lb) live pipis

2 tablespoons peanut oil

7 cm (3 in) knob ginger, finely sliced

5 garlic cloves, crushed

3 large red chillies, cut in half lengthways and deseeded

1 large red onion, cut in half and then into wedges

¼ cup shao hsing wine

1 tablespoon Chinese black vinegar

1 tablespoon oyster sauce

1 tablespoon light soy sauce

2 teaspoons white sugar

4 spring onions (scallions), trimmed and cut in half crossways

dash of sesame oil

pickled bamboo, poached chicken and lobster salad

When I created many of the recipes in this book it was Christmas-time. I was feeling particularly festive and indulgent, and I lost count of how many dinner parties I attended and held! Lobster (or crayfish, as it's often called in Australia) seemed to be on the menu rather frequently, as summer in Sydney is perfect seafood-eating weather, but you can easily substitute fresh prawns or crabmeat; as long as it's fresh, you can't go wrong. Talking of freshness, I always take advantage of the season for fresh bamboo – there is nothing more delicious in flavour and stunningly beautiful in a visual sense. You'll never go back to the tinned version. This recipe makes more pickled bamboo than you need, but it keeps for several weeks in the refrigerator and makes a lovely addition to salads, such as 'fresh mud crab salad' (page 66).

Place lobster in freezer for 1 hour, where it will 'go to sleep', then lower into a large stockpot of boiling salted water and cook for 5 minutes. Using tongs, carefully remove lobster, drain and allow to cool at room temperature.

Cut the horn-shaped bamboo shoot in half lengthways, strip off the outer fibrous layers and then trim about 2 cm (1 in) off the base. Cut bamboo into 5 mm (¼ in) wide strips and add to a pan of cold salted water. Bring to the boil and boil rapidly for 10 minutes. Drain and refresh bamboo under cold water. Repeat this process of boiling from a cold-water start, draining and refreshing twice more to remove any bitterness. To pickle the bamboo, place vinegar and sugar in a small pan, and stir over low heat, without boiling, until sugar is dissolved. Then simmer, uncovered and without stirring, for about 5 minutes, or until mixture is slightly reduced. Remove from stove, stir in fish sauce and the prepared bamboo.

To make the dressing, combine shallots, mustard, salt and lemon juice in a bowl. Stir in oil, vinegar and chervil and mix well.

To serve, remove meat from lobster and slice thickly on the diagonal. Slice chicken breasts thickly, also on the diagonal. Layer sliced lobster, chicken and pickled bamboo on a serving platter and spoon over the dressing. Sprinkle with a little pepper and drizzle with olive oil.

Serve as a starter for 4

1 × 700 g (1 lb 6 oz) live lobster

90 g (3 oz) pickled bamboo – see below

2 chicken breasts, from 'kylie's poached chicken' (page 190)

pinch cracked white pepper

dash of extra virgin olive oil

PICKLED BAMBOO

1 × 700 g (1 lb 6 oz) fresh bamboo shoot

⅓ cup rice wine vinegar

¼ cup white sugar

2 teaspoons fish sauce

SHALLOT, CHERVIL AND MUSTARD DRESSING

¼ cup finely diced red shallots

3 teaspoons Dijon mustard

½ teaspoon sea salt

2 tablespoons lemon juice

5 tablespoons extra virgin olive oil

1 teaspoon chardonnay vinegar

¼ cup finely chopped chervil

southern chinese-style squid

Serve as a starter for 4

The success of this recipe relies mainly on obtaining the freshest squid available – tender, silky strands of squid stir-fried with an array of wonderful salty and spicy aromatic ingredients. To finish the dish perfectly, all that's needed is a squeeze of fresh, sour lemon juice.

600 g (1¼ lb) small whole squid

¼ cup cornflour (cornstarch)

vegetable oil for deep-frying

1½ tablespoons finely sliced coriander stalks and roots

2 tablespoons finely sliced spring onions (scallions)

1 tablespoon finely diced ginger

1 tablespoon finely diced large red chillies, deseeded

1 tablespoon finely diced garlic

½ teaspoon sea salt

1 teaspoon Sichuan pepper and salt (page 194)

2 iceberg lettuce leaves, very finely sliced

2 lemons, cut in wedges

Clean the squid by gently pulling head and tentacles away from the body. Pull out the clear backbone (quill) from inside the body and discard entrails. Cut tentacles from the head just below the eyes; discard head. Remove side wings and fine membrane from body. Rinse the body, tentacles and wings thoroughly and pat dry with kitchen paper. Cut the squid down the centre so that it will open out flat, and slice the body and wings into 5 mm (¼ in) wide strips.

In a bowl, combine squid, including tentacles, with cornflour and toss to coat, shaking off any excess.

Heat oil in a hot wok until the surface seems to shimmer slightly. Add half the squid and deep-fry for about 1 minute, or until just tender and beginning to colour. Remove with a slotted spoon and drain well on kitchen paper. Repeat this process with remaining squid.

Pour off all but 1 tablespoon of oil from wok. Heat this until almost smoking, then add coriander, spring onions, ginger, chilli and garlic and stir-fry for 1 minute, or until fragrant. Return squid to wok with sea salt and half the Sichuan pepper and salt and stir-fry for a further 30 seconds.

To serve, place lettuce in a bowl, with lemon wedges on the side. Top with squid, sprinkle with remaining Sichuan pepper and salt and serve immediately.

roast wagyu beef fillet with blood plum sauce

You'll see that I've used Wagyu beef in a few of these recipes. I realise that it is only available at selected butchers and, even then, its price tag might make you faint, but let me explain my penchant for Wagyu beef. Quite simply, it's the best-tasting beef you can buy in Australia. It's grain-fed and is of such high quality that it's exported to Japan. Of course, you don't have to use Wagyu beef – all I'm saying is that you should use the best-quality, freshest beef you can lay your hands on.

Combine beef with kecap manis, wine, soy sauce, garlic and half the olive oil in a large bowl. Cover and refrigerate for 2 hours.

Preheat oven to 220°C (450°F). Remove beef from marinade and drain, reserving marinade. Heat remaining oil in a large frying pan and sear the beef on all sides until lightly browned. Transfer to a roasting tin and roast, uncovered, for 8 minutes. Pour over reserved marinade and roast for a further 3 minutes. Remove beef from oven, cover with foil and leave to rest in a warm place for 10 minutes.

Pour ¾ cup of the pan juices into a small frying pan and bring to the boil. Halve the plums, add to pan and simmer, uncovered, for about 5 minutes, or until plums are tender and the sauce is slightly reduced.

Finally, cut beef into 1 cm (½ in) thick slices and arrange on a platter. Spoon over blood plum sauce and sprinkle with Sichuan pepper and salt.

Serve as part of a banquet for 4

750 g (1½ lb) Wagyu beef fillet

⅓ cup kecap manis

⅓ cup shao hsing wine

2 tablespoons light soy sauce

6 garlic cloves, finely diced

½ cup extra virgin olive oil

350 g (11 oz) ripe blood plums – about 6

pinch Sichuan pepper and salt (page 194)

mussel salad with egg, tarragon and pickled cucumber

Serve as a starter for 4

This French-inspired salad is one of my all-time favourite recipes. The mussels are just barely cooked, so they remain juicy, plump, salty – absolutely gorgeous. The pickled cucumber is simple to make but intriguingly complex, adding a lovely depth of flavour to the salad, along with the unmistakeable, slightly aniseedy note of tarragon. And the boiled egg somehow brings the whole dish down to earth and balances the delicate textures of the mussels, herbs and cucumber.

750 g (1½ lb) live mussels

2 garlic cloves, crushed

2 tablespoons extra virgin olive oil

1 tablespoon roughly chopped tarragon

2 tablespoons roughly chopped flat-leaf parsley

4 hard-boiled free-range eggs

pinch cracked white pepper

STOCK

2 cups chicken stock (page 187)

2 cups white wine

1 spring onion (scallion), trimmed and sliced

¼ bunch flat-leaf parsley, cut in half crossways

1 teaspoon sea salt

1 teaspoon white sugar

1 teaspoon white peppercorns

4 bay leaves

PICKLED CUCUMBER

1 medium-sized cucumber, peeled

¼ cup chardonnay vinegar

1 teaspoon sea salt

1 teaspoon white sugar

Scrub, debeard, rinse and drain the mussels. Place all stock ingredients in a medium-sized, heavy-based pan and bring to the boil. Reduce heat and simmer, uncovered, until reduced by half. Increase heat and add mussels, stirring well to combine. As the mussels begin to open, immediately remove from pan with tongs and place in a bowl; discard any that won't open. (Take care not to overcook the mussels.) Remove the meat from the shells and set aside. Continue simmering the remaining stock over medium heat for a further 25 minutes, or until reduced by half again and richer in flavour.

Meanwhile, make the pickled cucumber. Cut cucumber in half lengthways and scoop out seeds. Place cut-side down on a chopping board and cut on the diagonal into 5 mm (¼ in) slices. Place in a bowl and combine with vinegar, salt and sugar. Cover and refrigerate for at least 1 hour.

Pound garlic, half the olive oil and a little sea salt with a pestle and mortar until you have a coarse paste. Gently stir into reserved mussel meat, along with herbs and a scant ¼ cup of reduced stock. Combine this with pickled cucumber.

Peel eggs, slice and arrange on a platter. Top with mussel and cucumber mixture, sprinkle with pepper and drizzle with remaining olive oil.

Influence and
Inspiration

I'd like to introduce you to billy kwong, my restaurant in Surry Hills, Sydney. Each night we 'smudge' our perfect little dining room by dry-roasting Sichuan peppercorns with sea salt in a hot wok. The aroma and smoke created not only smells divine but also 'cleanses' the air and energy of the space. I mean, can you imagine how cloudy the energy becomes in a place where, each night, seven days a week, for over three years, about a hundred different people hang out for a few hours?! The smudging ritual each evening is like an offering . . . and the Sichuan pepper and salt mix I use to smudge the restaurant I also use to marinate the duck for one of my signature dishes, crispy-skin duck with blood plum sauce (see over page).

The first night of shooting the TV series at billy kwong was very exciting and very scary! I invited friends, family and colleagues to join us in the restaurant – you see, it is rather confronting to have a camera crew breathing down your neck, saying, 'Can you just walk in the door again as if it's the first time you've been in here?' or 'Can you just crane your neck to the left because you're creating a shadow, but still try and look natural?' or 'Kylie, can you just create that flame again in your wok . . . without setting the kitchen on fire?'.

We wanted to capture the essence of billy kwong: dynamic, energetic, generous and a feast for the senses. We wanted people revelling in the warm, passionate atmosphere and eating delicious food – and we wanted a sense of the sublime madness and frantic pace in the kitchen. I remember saying to Nick, the floor manager, 'Now, Nick, what I need you and the waiters to do is completely bombard us; I want all the tables ordering at once, within 10 minutes or less.

AUGGHHHH!!!! What was I thinking? Three hours later, puffing, panting, swearing and screaming, I think we finally managed to feed everyone . . .

'Simon, did you manage to capture the spirit of b.k.?'

'Yes, Kyles, I think we did,' he sighed.

'Just as well,' I said, 'cos we're not going through that circus performance again!'

crispy-skin duck with blood plum sauce

This is one of the signature dishes at billy kwong. I remember a table of four once ordered four ducks because they'd heard so much about it – they wanted a duck each and that was that! If blood plums aren't in season, use blood oranges or regular oranges to add that lovely sourness.

Rinse duck under cold water. Trim away excess fat from inside and outside the cavity, but keep neck, parson's nose and winglets intact. Pat dry and rub the skin all over with Sichuan pepper and salt. Cover duck and place in refrigerator overnight to marinate.

Transfer duck to a large steamer basket. Place basket over a pan of boiling water and steam, covered with a tight-fitting lid, for about 1½ hours, or until the duck is cooked through (to test, insert a small knife between leg and breast – the juices should run clear). Using tongs, gently remove duck from steamer and place on a tray, breast-side up, to drain. Allow to cool slightly, then transfer to refrigerator to cool further.

Meanwhile, make the plum sauce. Combine water and sugar in a small pan and bring to the boil. Reduce heat to low and simmer, stirring occasionally, for about 5 minutes, or until slightly reduced. Add plums, fish sauce and spices and simmer for a further minute. Stir through lime juice and remove pan from stove. Keep the sauce warm while you fry the duck.

Place cooled duck breast-side up on a chopping board and, using a large knife or cleaver, cut duck in half lengthways through breastbone and backbone. Carefully ease meat away from carcass, leaving thighs, legs and wings intact. Lightly toss duck halves in flour to coat, shaking off any excess. Heat vegetable oil in a hot wok until the surface seems to shimmer slightly. Deep-fry duck halves, one at a time, for about 3 minutes, or until well browned and crispy. Using tongs, carefully remove duck from oil and drain well on kitchen paper, then leave to rest in a warm place for 5 minutes.

Finally, with a large knife or cleaver, slice the duck, arrange on a platter and spoon over the hot plum sauce.

Serve as part of a banquet for 6–8

1 × 1.5 kg (3 lb) duck

2 tablespoons Sichuan pepper and salt (page 194)

¼ cup plain (all-purpose) flour

vegetable oil for deep-frying

BLOOD PLUM SAUCE

1 cup water

1 cup white sugar

250 g (8 oz) ripe blood plums – about 4 – cut in half

⅔ cup fish sauce

6 whole star anise

2 cinnamon quills

⅓ cup lime juice

neil's chilli-salt squid

Serve as a starter for 4

In too many Chinese restaurants, chilli-salt squid is made from frozen squid – and it's often so salty that you can't stop drinking! What you're left with is an overall sense of cluttered and clumsy flavours. Working with Neil Perry at Rockpool really drummed into me the importance of freshness, and what I want to show you with this recipe of Neil's is how amazing chilli-salt squid is when it's done properly. So I use the freshest squid from South Australia, I test the chilli-salt to make sure it's not too salty and not too spicy, and I use fresh oil. This allows the natural integrity of the ingredients to come through, and then all you need is some aromatic spring onions and coriander, and a squeeze of lemon juice.

600 g (1¼ lb) small whole squid

⅓ cup plain (all-purpose) flour

1 tablespoon chilli powder

1 tablespoon sea salt

vegetable oil for deep-frying

2 large red chillies, cut in half lengthways and deseeded

2 tablespoons spring onion (scallion) julienne

¼ cup coriander sprigs

2 lemons, halved

Clean squid by gently pulling head and tentacles away from the body. Pull out the clear backbone (quill) from inside the body and discard entrails. Cut tentacles from the head just below the eyes; discard head. Remove side wings and fine membrane from body. Rinse body, tentacles and wings thoroughly and pat dry with kitchen paper. Cut squid down the centre so that it will open out flat, and slice body and wings into 5 mm (¼ in) wide strips.

In a large bowl, combine flour, chilli powder and salt. Add squid, including tentacles, and toss to coat, shaking off any excess flour.

Heat oil in a hot wok until the surface seems to shimmer slightly. Add half the squid and deep-fry for about 1 minute, or until just tender and beginning to colour. Remove with a slotted spoon and drain well on kitchen paper. Repeat process with remaining squid.

Add chillies to the same hot oil and fry for about 30 seconds, or until they are a deep bright-red colour; remove with a slotted spoon and drain well.

Arrange squid on a platter and garnish with fried chillies, spring onions and coriander. Serve immediately, with lemon halves.

hiramasa served raw, with sour, salty and fragrant dressing

The Australian yellowtail kingfish (*Seriola lalandi*) – 'hiramasa' is Japanese for kingfish – is a natural inhabitant of the waters off South Australia, where it is now farmed. Its firm flesh is full of flavour, and is superbly moist and silky. At billy kwong we buy the whole fish from our fishmonger and then fillet it ourselves, before serving it thinly sliced and raw, sashimi-style. This recipe is all about the beauty of fresh seafood – it is about having a product so fresh and so high in quality that you really shouldn't do too much to it. Make sure you use only the freshest, best-quality fish – and your sharpest knife to slice it into super-fine, beautiful sheets. If you can't get kingfish, substitute any other sashimi-grade fish fillets, such as tuna, salmon or swordfish. The fennel must be young and small, to ensure it will be sweet and tender.

Heat oil in a heavy-based pan, add onions and stir over medium heat for 1 minute. Add sugar and salt, reduce heat and simmer gently for 2 minutes, or until mixture starts to caramelise. Stir in vinegar and simmer for a further 30 seconds. Set aside.

Cut a slice from one end of the lemon. Stand the lemon cut-side down on a chopping board and, using a small, sharp knife, cut skin and pith away from flesh by slicing from top to bottom following the curve of the fruit. Slice between the membranes on either side of each segment to free it, then repeat with the remainder of the segments. Take care to remove all pith, otherwise the bitterness will interfere with the clean flavours of this dish.

Using a very sharp knife, cut fish into 5 mm (¼ in) slices and arrange on a platter. Top with lemon segments, fennel, capers and tomato. Spoon over the caramelised onions and garnish with fresh herbs and pepper.

Serve as a starter for 2

2 tablespoons extra virgin olive oil

2 salad onions, trimmed and finely sliced

1 tablespoon white sugar

1 teaspoon sea salt

1 tablespoon sherry vinegar

1 medium-sized lemon

200 g (6½ oz) sashimi-grade kingfish fillet

½ baby fennel bulb, trimmed and very finely sliced

2 teaspoons salted capers, rinsed and drained

1 small vine-ripened tomato, cut in half and finely sliced

2 teaspoons finely shredded flat-leaf parsley leaves

2 teaspoons finely shredded mint leaves

2 teaspoons picked chervil leaves

pinch cracked white pepper

stir-fried mussels with bean-thread vermicelli and black beans

Bean-thread vermicelli is made from mung-bean flour. Because the noodles become transparent when cooked, they are also called cellophane or glass noodles. They're available dried from Asian stores, and need only a brief soak in boiling water before being added to this stir-fry.

Scrub, debeard, rinse and drain mussels, then put in a wok with 1½ cups of cold water. Place over high heat, cover and steam until shells open. As mussels begin to open, immediately remove from wok with tongs and place in a bowl; discard any that won't open. Drain water from wok and wipe clean with kitchen paper.

Soak bean-thread vermicelli in boiling water for 3 minutes, or until softened; drain and set aside.

Remove seeds and membranes from capsicum. Cut into strips 1.5 cm (¾ in) wide, then cut each strip into squares.

Heat peanut oil in a hot wok and stir-fry spring onions, ginger, garlic, halved red chillies, onion, black beans and capsicum for 3 minutes, or until fragrant. Add mussels and drained vermicelli and stir-fry for a further 2 minutes. Pour shao hsing wine around sides of wok in a circular motion, then stir in sugar, oyster sauce, sesame oil, stock and bird's eye chillies; stir-fry for 3 minutes to create a rich sauce. Finally, add vinegar and coriander and serve immediately.

Serve as a starter for 4,
or as part of a banquet for 4–6

40 live mussels

90 g (3 oz) bean-thread vermicelli

½ red capsicum (bell pepper)

3 tablespoons peanut oil

7 spring onion (scallion) stems, cut into 5 cm (2 in) lengths

4 slices ginger

3 garlic cloves, crushed

3 large red chillies, cut in half lengthways and deseeded

1 small red onion, cut in half and then into wedges

2 tablespoons salted black beans

3 tablespoons shao hsing wine

2 teaspoons white sugar

2 tablespoons oyster sauce

½ teaspoon sesame oil

⅓ cup chicken stock (page 187)

2 bird's eye chillies, sliced

2 teaspoons Chinese black vinegar

handful of coriander sprigs

hamish's roast king george whiting with scallops and peperoncini

Serve as a main meal for 2

Hamish Ingham is a chef at billy kwong, and he is one of the most talented and most wonderful people I have ever worked beside.

Peperoncini are red, thin chillies that are mostly sold pickled for antipasto – try to find Monferrato brand.

1 medium-sized red capsicum (bell pepper)

4–6 tablespoons extra virgin olive oil

2 medium-sized vine-ripened tomatoes

8 sea scallops on the half-shell

1 medium-sized salad onion, finely sliced

1 garlic clove, finely diced

4 peperoncini, drained and cut in half

2 teaspoons finely sliced preserved lemon rind

juice of 1 lemon

1/3 cup basil leaves

pinch cracked white pepper and sea salt

2–3 whole King George whiting or sole – about 700 g (1 lb 6 oz) in total – scaled and cleaned

Preheat oven to 200°C (400°F). Place capsicum in a roasting tin and drizzle with a little olive oil. Roast, uncovered, for about 20 minutes, or until skin blisters and blackens, turning once halfway through cooking time. Transfer capsicum to a bowl, cover with plastic wrap and leave to stand for 10 minutes. Peel skin from capsicum, cut in half and remove seeds and membranes. Slice flesh into 5 mm (1/4 in) strips and set aside. Cut tomatoes into quarters, discarding seeds and juices, then cut each quarter lengthways into thirds.

Clean scallops and cut them away from the shell, keeping the coral intact. Heat 1–2 tablespoons of olive oil in a medium-sized frying pan, add scallops and cook for about 30 seconds on each side, or until lightly browned and just cooked through. Remove from pan and cover with foil to keep warm. Add 1 tablespoon of olive oil to the same pan and place over medium heat. Add onion and garlic, and cook, stirring occasionally, for 1 minute, or until onion has softened. Add peperoncini and cook for a further minute. Return scallops to pan, along with reserved tomato, capsicum, another tablespoon of olive oil, preserved lemon rind, lemon juice, basil, pepper and salt. Stir to combine, then remove from heat. Keep warm while you cook the fish.

Reduce oven temperature to 180°C (350°F). Cook the fish in a heated, oiled frying pan until lightly browned on both sides. Transfer to a roasting tin and roast, uncovered, for about 8 minutes, or until the fish is just cooked through when tested: the flesh should be white through to the bone. Remove from oven, cover with foil and leave in a warm place for 3 minutes. Arrange fish on a platter, top with scallop and peperoncini mixture and drizzle with a little olive oil.

italian mushroom ragout – inspired by franca and stefano manfredi

During my cooking career I have had the pleasure of working with some of the most inspiring and original people. How I loved my time working with Stefano and Franca Manfredi in their very special, small, intimate, intense kitchen at The Restaurant Manfredi. To me, this scrumptious mushroom recipe symbolises the Manfredi family: down-to-earth, full of substance, elegant, vibrant and comforting. This ragout is delicious simply served with crusty bread, or as a side dish to accompany roasted poultry or meat. You should be able to get most of the mushroom varieties in leading supermarkets and selected fruit and vegetable stores. If you can't find them all, just use a selection of what's available.

Place garlic, onions and salt in a heavy-based pan. Cover with all the mushrooms except enoki and cloud ear fungus. Top with butter, olive oil and pepper and place over high heat for 5 minutes, without stirring, to allow the flavours of the onions and garlic to penetrate the mushrooms.

Add wine and remaining mushrooms, stirring to combine. Reduce heat and simmer, uncovered, for about 5 minutes, or until mushrooms are just tender. Stir in parsley and serve.

Serve as part of a banquet for 4–6

8 garlic cloves, crushed

4 salad onions, trimmed and finely sliced

1 tablespoon sea salt

200 g (6½ oz) fresh button mushrooms

100 g (3½ oz) fresh oyster mushrooms

150 g (5 oz) fresh shiitake mushrooms, stems discarded

100 g (3½ oz) fresh Swiss brown mushrooms

100 g (3½ oz) fresh enoki mushrooms

100 g (3½ oz) fresh black cloud ear fungus

125 g (4 oz) unsalted butter, roughly chopped

½ cup extra virgin olive oil

pinch cracked white pepper

½ cup dry white wine

½ cup roughly chopped flat-leaf parsley

danielle's creamy polenta with anchovy, olive and fresh tomato sauce

Serve as a starter for 4, or a light meal for 2

Danielle Renwick is a chef at billy kwong. I was first struck by her extraordinary focus and attention to detail at Rockpool and Wockpool – it's simply a beautiful thing to watch Danielle cook. Since then we have worked together for more than 10 years, and I'm delighted to include one of her favourite recipes in my book.

2 medium-sized red capsicums (bell peppers)

½ cup extra virgin olive oil

3 cups milk

¾ cup water

200 g (6½ oz) polenta

50 g (1½ oz) unsalted butter, chopped

⅔ cup finely grated parmesan

4 garlic cloves, finely sliced

10 anchovies

sea salt and cracked white pepper

2 medium-sized vine-ripened tomatoes, roughly chopped

½ cup pitted black olives, coarsely chopped

1½ cups flat-leaf parsley leaves

5 tablespoons red wine vinegar

Preheat oven to 200°C (400°F). Place capsicums in a roasting tin and drizzle with 1 tablespoon of the olive oil. Roast, uncovered, for about 20 minutes, or until skin blisters and blackens, turning once halfway through cooking time. Transfer capsicums to a bowl, cover with plastic wrap and leave to stand for 10 minutes. Peel skin from capsicums, cut in half and remove seeds and membranes. Slice flesh into 5 cm (2 in) strips and set aside.

Combine milk and water in a heavy-based pan and bring to the boil. Gradually add polenta, whisking continuously. Reduce heat to low and cook, stirring regularly with a wooden spoon, for about 30 minutes, or until polenta is soft and thickened. Stir in butter, parmesan, remaining olive oil, 1 teaspoon of salt and a pinch of cracked pepper.

Meanwhile, heat half the remaining olive oil in a frying pan, add garlic, anchovies, ¼ teaspoon of salt and a pinch of pepper and cook, stirring occasionally, over medium heat for about 3 minutes, or until garlic is soft and translucent. Add tomatoes, reserved capsicums and olives and cook for a further 15 minutes, or until the tomatoes begin to break down. Stir in parsley and vinegar and remove from stove.

To serve, spoon polenta into individual bowls and top with warm tomato, anchovy and olive sauce. Serve immediately.

baked whole snapper filled with lobster and lemongrass, served with roast cherry tomatoes

When whole snapper is baked slowly, it has a really silky, soft texture. This recipe uses an intriguing blend of Asian and Western ingredients: the filling is flavoured with lemongrass, spring onions, garlic and ginger, while the roast tomatoes are caramelised with tarragon and olive oil. The lobster stuffing is admittedly rather indulgent, but you can always substitute prawns or a fillet of white fish.

Preheat oven to 150°C (300°F). Place cherry tomatoes in a roasting tin, drizzle with half the olive oil and sprinkle with tarragon sprigs, pepper and half the salt. Cover tin with foil and roast for 30 minutes. Remove foil and roast for a further 5 minutes, or until tomatoes are soft and wilted. Remove tomatoes from oven and set aside to cool slightly before drizzling with vinegar and sprinkling with remaining salt.

Meanwhile, put all stuffing ingredients in a bowl and mix well. Pat fish dry with kitchen paper and place on a large, oiled oven tray. Fill fish cavity with stuffing mixture, drizzle with the remaining olive oil and sprinkle with a little pepper. Cover tray with foil and bake for 15 minutes. Remove foil and roast for a further 20 minutes, or until fish is just cooked through when tested. The flesh should be white through to the bone. If the flesh is still translucent, cook for another minute or so.

Carefully slide the fish into a large, shallow bowl. Pour over reserved tomatoes with their pan juices and garnish with lemongrass and chilli. Serve immediately.

Serve as part of a banquet for 4

250 g (8 oz) cherry tomatoes

¾ cup extra virgin olive oil

½ bunch tarragon

cracked white pepper

2 teaspoons sea salt

1 tablespoon red wine vinegar

1 × 750 g (1½ lb) whole snapper, scaled, cleaned and gutted

1 tablespoon very finely sliced lemongrass, cut on the diagonal

1 tablespoon finely sliced large red chilli

LOBSTER AND LEMONGRASS STUFFING

280 g (9 oz) fresh uncooked lobster meat, roughly chopped

2 tablespoons finely diced lemongrass

¼ cup finely sliced spring onions (scallions)

2 garlic cloves, finely diced

1 tablespoon finely diced ginger

1 tablespoon red wine vinegar

1 tablespoon extra virgin olive oil

1 tablespoon light soy sauce

1 teaspoon white sugar

stir-fried black-lip abalone with young ginger and fresh shiitake mushrooms

Abalone, a mollusc found in southern Australian waters and throughout the Pacific, is an absolute delicacy in Chinese cuisine. Black-lip abalone is distinguished by its black lip and the deep, outward-radiating grooves on the outside of its shell. I just adore abalone's extraordinary texture – it is silky, chewy, tender, firm, delicate and dense all at once – and I love this stir-fry for its interesting textural combinations and its sheer deliciousness. If yellow garlic chives are unavailable, use regular garlic chives.

To shuck the abalone, place the tip of a sharp knife in a thin part of the shell and ease underneath flesh, working the knife down until the whole muscle is freed from the shell. Lift out flesh, remove the attached gut and wash well. Reserve shell to serve abalone in later. Cut away tough lip from abalone and discard. Place abalone on a chopping board with the side that was attached to the shell facing upwards and, using a very sharp knife, slice the abalone very finely.

Heat peanut oil in a hot wok until the surface seems to shimmer slightly, then stir-fry abalone for 10 seconds. Immediately remove from wok, using a slotted spoon, and set aside.

Add garlic and ginger to wok and stir-fry for 30 seconds, or until fragrant. Add wine, mushrooms, chives, sugar, soy sauce, oyster sauce and chicken stock and stir-fry for 1 minute. Quickly return abalone to wok, along with vinegar, sesame oil, shallots, half the lettuce and half the spring onions.

Place remaining lettuce in centre of plate and top with cleaned abalone shell. Spoon abalone stir-fry into shell and garnish with remaining spring onions. Serve immediately.

Serve with steamed rice as a main meal for 2

1 × 600 g (1¼ lb) live abalone

⅓ cup peanut oil

2 garlic cloves, finely diced

2 tablespoons finely diced ginger

2 tablespoons shao hsing wine

½ cup fresh black cloud ear fungus

½ cup very finely sliced fresh shiitake mushroom caps

⅓ bunch yellow garlic chives, cut into thirds crossways

1½ teaspoons white sugar

1 tablespoon light soy sauce

2 teaspoons oyster sauce

1 tablespoon chicken stock (page 187)

1 teaspoon Chinese black vinegar

dash of sesame oil

¼ cup finely sliced red shallots

½ cup finely shredded iceberg lettuce leaves

¼ cup spring onion (scallion) julienne

jodie's fresh fig, raspberry and almond cake

Jodie Tilse was the recipe writer for my first book, as well as this one, and without her I simply would not feel confident sharing my recipes with people. I love her delightful personality – she has this wonderful balance of easygoingness, warmth and generosity paired with staggering attention to detail and astonishing precision. I felt very honoured and excited when Jodie agreed to let me have one of her favourite recipes for this book. I like the sweet, musky flavours of fresh figs and raspberries in this cake, offset by the slight bitterness of the orange.

Preheat oven to 180°C (350°F). Lightly grease a 23 cm (9 in) round cake tin and line the base and sides with a double thickness of baking paper to extend 2 cm (¾ in) above the sides.

Remove stems from figs and cut lengthways into 5 mm (¼ in) slices.

Sift icing sugar and flour into a large bowl. Stir in almond meal and orange zest until well combined. Place egg whites in a bowl and whisk lightly with a fork for a few seconds until egg white breaks down slightly. Add egg whites, melted butter and milk to almond mixture and stir until just combined. Fold through half the raspberries, being careful not to over-mix the cake.

Pour half the cake mixture into prepared pan and scatter with half the remaining berries. Pour remaining cake mixture over the berries. Arrange sliced figs on top, pushing the slices into the cake mixture on a slight angle. Scatter over remaining berries, *gently* pressing them partly into cake mixture, then sprinkle evenly with demerara sugar.

Bake cake for about 1 hour and 15 minutes, or until a skewer inserted in the centre comes out clean. If cake is becoming too brown, cover loosely with foil.

Leave cake in its tin for 10 minutes before turning onto a wire rack. Serve warm or cold, with a dollop of cream.

Serves 8–10

2 medium-sized fresh figs

2 cups icing (confectioner's) sugar

⅔ cup self-raising (self-rising) flour

2 cups almond meal (ground almonds)

1 tablespoon finely grated orange zest

8 egg whites

185 g (6 oz) butter, melted

1½ tablespoons milk

200 g (6½ oz) fresh raspberries

1½ teaspoons demerara sugar

thick or clotted cream, to serve

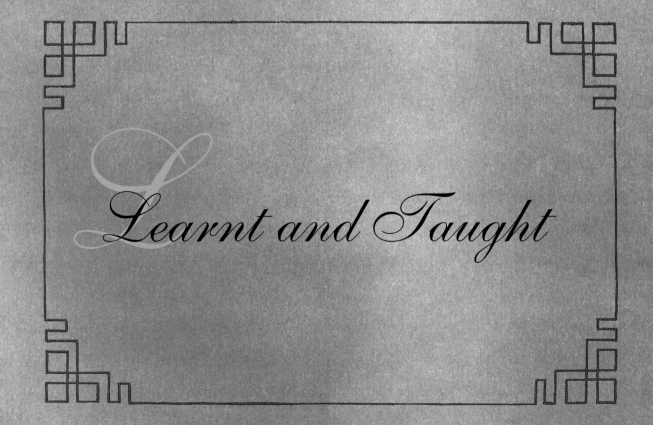

Learnt and Taught

Let me tell you about filming a segment with my mum and my little niece, Indy (short for Indiana!). When I was Indy's age, my mum used to make these pink jelly cakes (see recipe on page 74), and we wanted to show how such rituals – and a love of food – are handed down from generation to generation.

Well, the week before, we had a family dinner, and my mother, being my mother, was sitting next to Indy, and we were all talking about making jelly cakes on the TV show, when Mum says to Indy, 'Now, just remember, darling, when you go on Auntie Kylie's set, you're not allowed to stick your fingers in the bowl and lick them and everything.' And I went, 'Mum, be quiet! That's precisely what Simon and I want her to do. We want her to be as natural as possible.' Aren't parents funny? All we wanted was to have little Indy with her fingers stuck in the bowl, then getting her hands all covered in coconut and everything.

We needn't have worried. Indy turned out to be a natural performer and actress; she had the TV crew in absolute stitches! She took great delight in sitting in Auntie Kylie's 'big' make-up chair while she had her hair fussed over and plaited with little pink elastics, and had a touch of sparkly rouge dabbed on her cheeks. She wore the sweetest butterfly shirt, and the smallest, cutest, bluest hipster jeans. We were all amazed at her ability to just be herself. I mean, when you do television the whole thing is to try and act as natural as possible – and that's exactly what we adults find the hardest thing to do at times.

I found myself musing about how Indy has made jelly cakes with my mum before, so she'll make them as a child and later as a grown-up woman, and then eventually will probably teach her own children how to make them. It's all about generations, and about women – about mothers and daughters and grand-daughters and aunties.

delicious fried rice

Fried rice is one of those lovely comforting foods that everyone in the world seems to like – no one is intimidated by fried rice. Somehow all these rogue ingredients have crept into restaurant versions over the years, such as corn, peas, ham and the like. I find the trick with fried rice is to keep it really simple and traditional – just some really fresh and fluffy eggs, onion, bacon or Chinese sausage, ginger and some spring onions.

Heat oil in a hot wok until the surface seems to shimmer slightly. Pour beaten eggs into wok and cook for about 1 minute, lightly scrambling them and rotating the wok to ensure even cooking. When almost cooked through, carefully remove omelette from wok with a fish slice and drain on kitchen paper. Set aside.

Wipe out wok with kitchen paper, add extra oil and stir-fry ginger and garlic for 1 minute, or until very aromatic. Add onion and stir-fry for 2 minutes, or until lightly browned and tender. Add bacon and stir-fry for a further minute, or until lightly browned. Stir in sugar and wine, then stir-fry for 30 seconds. Finally, add rice, reserved omelette, oyster sauce, spring onions, Maggi seasoning and sesame oil. Stir-fry for 3 minutes, or until rice is heated through. Roughly chop omelette into smaller pieces as you stir.

Divide rice between individual bowls and garnish with extra spring onions. Combine soy sauce and chilli in a small bowl and serve on the side.

Serve as a simple supper for 2–4, or as part of a banquet for 6

⅓ cup peanut oil

4 large free-range eggs, beaten

1 tablespoon peanut oil, extra

1½ tablespoons finely chopped ginger

4 garlic cloves, diced

1 medium-sized brown onion, finely diced

½ cup roughly chopped rindless bacon rashers or Chinese sausage

1 teaspoon white sugar

2 tablespoons shao hsing wine

5 cups cooked medium-grain white rice

1 tablespoon oyster sauce

1 cup finely sliced spring onions (scallions)

3 teaspoons Maggi seasoning

¼ teaspoon sesame oil

2 spring onions (scallions), finely sliced on the diagonal

¼ cup light soy sauce

½ large red chilli, finely sliced on the diagonal

hokkien noodles four ways

To me, Hokkien noodles symbolise childhood in the Kwong household. They take me back to a time when Mum and Dad were working very, very hard in order to give me and my two brothers, Paul and Jamie, the best possible education and opportunities. Because life was so hectic, Mum cleverly taught us how to cook so that we could help her and Dad with the day-to-day running of the family. Stir-fried Hokkien noodles with chicken seemed to be the easiest, most comforting and economical way of feeding a very hungry, growing family. We each developed our own distinctive style – and now I can't wait until my niece, Indy, and her two little brothers, Jye and Fin, are old enough and tall enough to cook their own versions of this Kwong family favourite.

mum's hokkien noodles

Of course, all our Hokkien noodle dishes are variations of the original recipe, Mum's. Her Hokkien noodles are very simple: quickly executed and very delicious.

There was no time for playing around with flavours like I do, because she had a family to feed, a household to run and work to get done!

Serve as a simple lunch or supper for 2, or as part of a banquet for 4–6

Combine ginger, sherry, cornflour, sugar, sesame oil and half the soy sauce in a bowl. Add chicken and, using your hands, mix well. Cover and refrigerate for 1 hour.

Blanch noodles in boiling salted water until 'al dente' – about 4 minutes. Drain, refresh in cold water, then thoroughly drain again.

Trim ends from choy sum, then cut crossways into three and wash well; drain.

Heat oil in a hot wok until the surface seems to shimmer slightly, then stir-fry chicken for 1 minute. Add mushrooms, onion and carrot and stir-fry for 1 minute. Add oyster sauce and water and stir-fry for 30 seconds. Finally, add noodles, choy sum, spring onions and remaining soy sauce and stir-fry for about 2 minutes, or until chicken is just cooked through and noodles are hot. Arrange in bowls and serve immediately.

2 tablespoons finely diced ginger

1 tablespoon dry sherry

1 teaspoon cornflour (cornstarch)

½ teaspoon white sugar

dash of sesame oil

1 tablespoon light soy sauce

2 free-range chicken breast fillets, thickly sliced on the diagonal

600 g (1¼ lb) fresh Hokkien noodles

½ bunch choy sum

¼ cup peanut oil

⅓ cup finely sliced 'braised dried chinese mushrooms' (page 186)

1 large white onion, cut in half and then into thick wedges

1 medium carrot, cut into julienne

1 tablespoon oyster sauce

2 tablespoons water

5 spring onions (scallions), trimmed and cut into 10 cm (4 in) lengths

paul's hokkien noodles

Serve as a simple lunch or supper for 2, or as part of a banquet for 4–6

Paul Kwong's Hokkien noodle dish is gorgeous, with lots of fresh, vibrant vegetables in it, including red capsicum and eggplant. His version is very colourful and flamboyant, just like him. Paul regularly cooks this for his dinner parties.

¼ cup shao hsing wine

2 tablespoons light soy sauce

2 teaspoons white sugar

2 tablespoons hoisin sauce

dash of sesame oil

3 garlic cloves, roughly chopped

2 free-range chicken breast fillets, thickly sliced on the diagonal

½ medium-sized eggplant (aubergine)

600 g (1¼ lb) fresh Hokkien noodles

⅓ cup peanut oil

2 sticks of celery, finely sliced on the diagonal

¾ cup red capsicum (bell pepper) julienne

2 tablespoons finely diced ginger

¼ cup water

1 tablespoon oyster sauce

5 spring onions (scallions), trimmed and cut into 10 cm (4 in) lengths

Combine half the wine, half the soy sauce and half the sugar in a large bowl. Add hoisin sauce, sesame oil and garlic and mix well. Add chicken and, using your hands, mix thoroughly to combine. Cover and refrigerate for 1 hour.

Cut eggplant in half lengthways and finely slice on the diagonal.

Blanch noodles in boiling salted water until 'al dente' – about 4 minutes. Drain, refresh in cold water, then drain again thoroughly.

Heat half the oil in a hot wok until the surface seems to shimmer slightly, then stir-fry chicken for about 2 minutes, or until almost cooked. Remove from wok and set aside. Heat remaining oil until hot and stir-fry eggplant, celery, capsicum and ginger for 1 minute. Add remaining wine and simmer for 30 seconds, followed by the water, oyster sauce and remaining sugar and soy sauce; stir-fry for 1 minute. Add noodles and stir-fry for a further minute. Finally, return chicken to wok with spring onions and stir-fry until chicken is just cooked through and noodles are hot. Arrange noodles in bowls and serve immediately.

jamie's hokkien noodles

Jamie Kwong's Hokkien noodles are very carefully prepared – the choy sum is cooked separately with some garlic and salt and then set aside. The chicken is perfectly cooked, and the lovely twist of the braised Chinese mushrooms give the dish a really beautiful flavour. This recipe always reminds me of Jamie's careful approach to life and his gentle, articulate manner.

Trim ends from choy sum, then cut crossways into quarters. Wash thoroughly and drain.

Blanch noodles in boiling salted water until 'al dente' – about 4 minutes. Drain noodles, cover with foil and keep warm.

Heat half the oil in a hot wok until the surface seems to shimmer slightly. Add salt to the hot oil, immediately toss in choy sum and stir-fry for 30 seconds. Add garlic and stir-fry for 1 minute. Remove choy sum from wok and set aside.

In a clean wok, heat remaining oil and stir-fry chicken for 2 minutes. Add mushrooms, ginger, spring onions, wine, water, oyster sauce, sugar, soy sauce and sesame oil and stir-fry for a further minute. Return choy sum to wok and stir-fry for 30 seconds.

Arrange noodles in bowls, top with chicken and vegetables, and serve immediately.

Serve as a simple lunch or supper for 2, or as part of a banquet for 4–6

½ bunch choy sum

600 g (1¼ lb) fresh Hokkien noodles

5 tablespoons peanut oil

½ teaspoon sea salt

2 garlic cloves, finely diced

2 free-range chicken breast fillets, thickly sliced on the diagonal

½ cup finely sliced 'braised dried chinese mushrooms' (page 186)

2 tablespoons ginger julienne

5 spring onions (scallions), trimmed and cut into 10 cm (4 in) lengths

¼ cup shao hsing wine

2 tablespoons water

1 tablespoon oyster sauce

1 teaspoon white sugar

1 teaspoon light soy sauce

dash of sesame oil

kylie's hokkien noodles

Serve as a simple lunch or supper for 2, or as part of a banquet for 4–6

My Hokkien noodles are, I guess, like me – they're a bit radical! They've got all my favourite ingredients in them: Chinese black vinegar, luscious kecap manis, sesame oil, shao hsing wine and a little bit of sugar, as well as pickles and mint. And I just love eating them with chillies. Again you can see the recurring theme in Asian cooking of each dish being a balance of sweet, sour, salty and hot flavours. In this recipe I've used organic chicken breast fillets, but any good-quality chicken is fine. I like to leave the skin on, to keep the chicken moist.

5 tablespoons roughly chopped ginger

4 garlic cloves, crushed

⅓ cup kecap manis

2 tablespoons Chinese black vinegar

2 tablespoons Maggi seasoning

⅔ cup shao hsing wine

2 organic chicken breast fillets, thickly sliced on the diagonal

600 g (1¼ lb) fresh Hokkien noodles

2 tablespoons peanut oil

1 small cucumber, peeled and finely sliced on the diagonal

¾ cup carrot and onion pickles (page 132)

2 tablespoons oyster sauce

⅔ cup fresh black cloud ear fungus

¼ cup mint leaves

pinch Sichuan pepper and salt (page 194)

Pound ginger and garlic with a pestle and mortar until you have a coarse paste. Combine half the paste in a bowl with kecap manis, vinegar, Maggi seasoning and half the wine. Add chicken and, using your hands, mix thoroughly. Cover and refrigerate for 1 hour.

Meanwhile, blanch noodles in boiling salted water until 'al dente' – about 4 minutes. Drain, refresh in cold water, then thoroughly drain again and set aside.

Heat oil in a hot wok until the surface seems to shimmer slightly, then stir-fry chicken for about 2 minutes, or until almost cooked. Remove from wok and set aside. Add remaining ginger and garlic paste, cucumber and noodles and stir-fry for 1 minute. Add remaining wine, pickled vegetables, oyster sauce and mushrooms and stir-fry for a further minute. Return chicken to wok and stir-fry until chicken is just cooked through and noodles are hot.

Stir mint leaves through noodles. Arrange in bowls, sprinkle with Sichuan pepper and salt, and serve immediately.

fresh mud crab salad

This is a light, summery dish that's refreshing to eat on a hot day. I just love the sweet, delicate flavour of fresh crabmeat. The addition of pickled bamboo gives the salad depth of flavour, the vinegar balances out the sweetness of the bamboo and the coriander gives a lovely freshness to the salad. If you don't want the hassle of buying a live crab, cooking it and picking out the meat, then by all means buy ready-picked crabmeat – it's more expensive, but it'll save you a lot of preparation time.

Place crab in freezer for 1 hour, where it will 'go to sleep', then lower into a large stockpot of boiling salted water and cook for 5 minutes. Using tongs, carefully remove the crab from the pot, drain and allow to cool at room temperature.

Twist claws and legs from crab and pull off the top shell. Crack the large claws with the back of a heavy knife or cleaver and extract the meat. Cut along the small legs with scissors, then break them in half and extract the meat. Discard the bony section at the head, rinse body cavity and under the shell where the legs were attached. Cut body of crab into quarters. Using a skewer, extract ('pick') meat from each piece of body, removing any cartilage. When all the meat has been picked, discard all shell and any stray fragments of cartilage. You should have about 200 g (6½ oz) of cooked, picked crabmeat.

Place crabmeat in a bowl and gently combine with the remaining ingredients except olive oil and pepper. Serve salad in bowls, drizzled with olive oil and sprinkled with pepper.

Serve as a starter for 2–4

1 × 750 g (1½ lb) mud crab or blue crab

2 teaspoons finely diced ginger

¼ cup finely sliced red shallots

¼ cup finely sliced spring onions (scallions), green part only

2 tablespoons roughly chopped coriander leaves

2 tablespoons finely sliced fresh black cloud ear fungus

45 g (1½ oz) pickled bamboo (page 20), cut into julienne

½ teaspoon red wine vinegar

¼ teaspoon sea salt

1 tablespoon extra virgin olive oil

pinch cracked white pepper

live tasmanian scallops barely roasted, served with mint

I'm lucky enough to be able to get freshly harvested Tasmanian scallops. They're still alive, and have to be shucked open like oysters. They're the most beautiful things you've ever seen or tasted; because the waters off Tasmania are so clean, the scallops have a lovely salty-sweet flavour. If you can't find live scallops, just get the freshest scallops you can lay your hands on. Because these scallops are naturally so delicious, the less you do to them, the better – I just barely roast them with a drizzle of extra virgin olive oil and a sprinkling of salt, followed by a splash of balsamic vinegar and some fresh mint. It doesn't get any better than that.

Preheat oven to 220°C (450°F). Clean scallops and their shells, leaving scallop attached. Arrange scallops on a baking dish, sprinkle with the salt and half the olive oil.

Roast scallops for 4 minutes, being careful not to overcook them. Drizzle with vinegar and remaining olive oil. Garnish with mint and pepper and serve immediately.

Serve as a starter for 4

12 live sea scallops

½ teaspoon sea salt

2 tablespoons extra virgin olive oil

1 tablespoon balsamic vinegar

2 teaspoons finely shredded mint leaves

pinch cracked white pepper

red-braised beef chuck with chinese marbled eggs

Beef chuck is a beautiful, inexpensive cut of meat that lends itself to slow braising. When cooked, the meat not only falls apart in your mouth, but also is embraced by the wonderful flavours of star anise, ginger and cinnamon. Coupled with the pretty marbled eggs, this is the ultimate warming and comforting dish.

Gently tap the eggs on a hard surface to crack the shell slightly all over, but do not peel.

In a large stockpot, bring red-braising stock to the boil. Lower eggs and beef into simmering stock, ensuring they are fully submerged. Braise very gently, covered, for 1 hour and 40 minutes, or until the meat is soft and gelatinous, skimming stock regularly with a ladle.

Remove pot from stove. Using tongs, remove beef and eggs from stock and drain well. Peel eggs.

To serve, arrange beef and eggs on a platter and ladle over some of the hot stock. Finally, sprinkle the dish with Sichuan pepper.

Serve as part of a banquet for 4–6

6 hard-boiled eggs

1 quantity red-braising stock (page 192)

1.75 kg (3½ lb) beef chuck, cut into 5 cm (2 in) thick slices

pinch Sichuan pepper

gently poached pigeon served with scallop and black cloud ear fungus salad

Serve as a starter for 2

We Chinese just adore pigeon, with its richly flavoured, dense, silky-textured flesh. This silkiness and integrity of flavour is preserved by poaching, a very gentle way of cooking. The pigeon is perfectly balanced by the lovely, light, zingy, fresh salad of citrus and chilli.

1 quantity white-poaching stock (page 195)

1 × 500 g (1 lb) pigeon (squab)

½ cup finely sliced salad onions

1 teaspoon white sugar

½ teaspoon sea salt

2 tablespoons extra virgin olive oil

8 sea scallops on the half-shell

½ cup fresh black cloud ear fungus

¼ cup lime juice

½ large red chilli, finely sliced on the diagonal

1 teaspoon fish sauce

In a large stockpot, bring white-poaching stock to the boil. Meanwhile, rinse pigeon under cold water, then trim away excess fat from inside and outside the cavity. Keep neck, parson's nose and winglets intact, but remove wingtips and claws. Lower pigeon breast-side down into simmering stock, ensuring it is fully submerged. Poach very gently for exactly 9 minutes. Remove pot from stove and allow pigeon to steep in the stock for 2 hours at room temperature to complete the cooking process. Using tongs, gently remove pigeon from stock, being careful not to tear the breast skin. Place pigeon breast-side up on a wire rack over a tray, to drain and cool.

In a bowl, combine onions with sugar and salt, mix well and leave to stand for 30 minutes. Add cloud ear fungus, lime juice, chilli and fish sauce and set aside.

Remove head and neck of pigeon and discard. Remove wings, cut in half, and reserve for later. Place pigeon breast-side up on a chopping board and cut on either side of the breastbone to remove each half in one piece. Heat olive oil in a heavy-based frying pan and sear pigeon halves all over until lightly browned and crispy. Remove and drain well.

Clean scallops and cut them away from the shell, keeping the coral intact. Add scallops to a lightly oiled frying pan and sear for about 1 minute on each side, or until lightly browned and just cooked through. Remove from pan.

To serve, separate pigeon thighs from breasts, then slice breasts in half on the diagonal. Place reserved wings in the centre of a platter and top with onion mixture. Arrange remaining pigeon on top and garnish with scallops.

mum's jelly cakes

When I was little, Mum used to make these incredible jelly cakes. It's really quite funny, because of course we're Chinese and yet we're making these very Australian cakes. They're basically little patty-pan cakes rolled first in red jelly that's still wobbly and then in desiccated coconut. I guess they're like a pretty-in-pink version of the all-Australian lamington – and I still have no idea where my mother got the recipe from . . .

Pour boiling water into a large heatproof jug. Sprinkle jelly crystals into jug, stir until crystals are dissolved, then stir in cold water. Pour jelly mixture into a large, shallow dish, about 20 × 25 cm (8 × 10 in), cover and refrigerate for 2–2½ hours, or until jelly is just starting to set. (It is important that the jelly is used at the right consistency; if it is too firm it will not stick to the cakes.)

Meanwhile, lightly grease 3 × 12-hole shallow patty-pan tins (1½-tablespoon capacity) and preheat oven to 180°C (350°F). Cream together butter and sugar with an electric mixer until light and fluffy. Add egg and beat until just combined. Add flour, milk and vanilla and mix until smooth.

Spoon tablespoons of the mixture into prepared tins. Bake for about 10 minutes, or until lightly browned. They're ready when a skewer inserted in the centre comes out clean. Remove cakes from tins and transfer to a wire rack to cool.

Remove jelly from refrigerator and quickly roll a cake in the jelly, coating it evenly. Toss the jelly-covered cake in coconut until it's coated all over. Repeat with remaining cakes and arrange on a platter to serve.

Makes about 30 little cakes

1 cup boiling water

1 × 85 g (3 oz) packet strawberry or raspberry jelly crystals

¾ cup cold water

125 g (4 oz) butter

½ cup caster (superfine) sugar

1 egg

1¼ cups self-raising (self-rising) flour, sifted

½ cup milk

½ teaspoon vanilla essence

2½ cups desiccated coconut

Necessity and Generosity

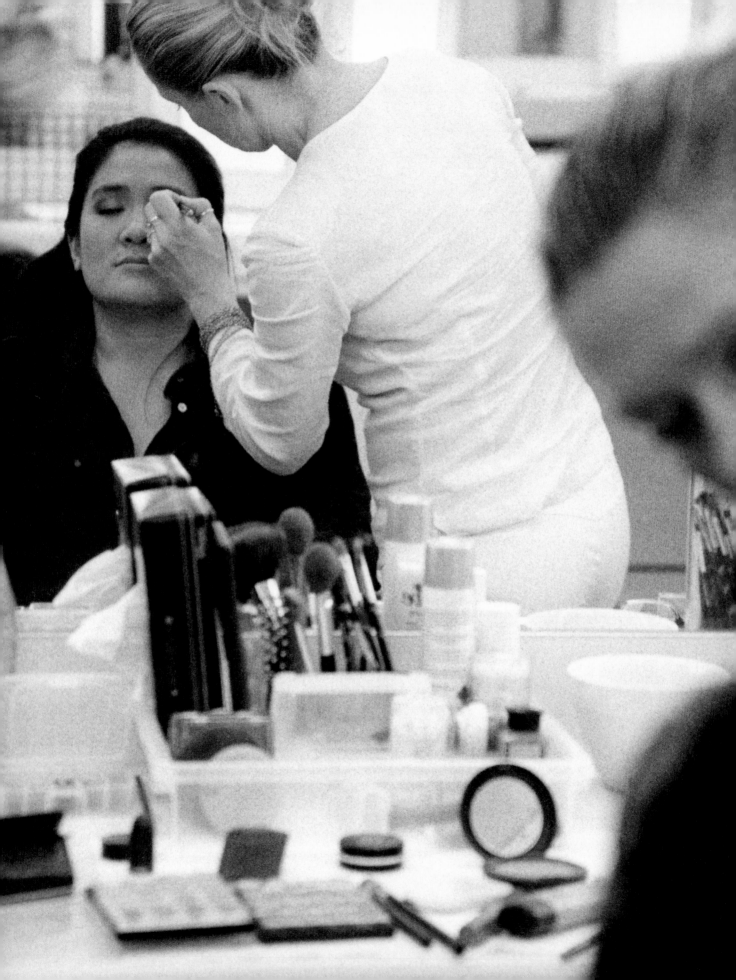

It is action-packed, this weird, mad, chaotic and wonderful world of television and sets and studios and props and, oh, my goodness, just so many people everywhere. I thought I had a lot of bodies running around at billy kwong, but you should see the number of people running around a telly set! There's the producer/director, of course; the D.A., director's assistant; two cameramen and one assistant; the floor manager; the set designer; the safety officer; the food stylist; a chef and a kitchenhand; and an associate producer/researcher. Weaving in between everyone is a man called Chicka, who adjusts all the lighting and has black gaffa tape stuck to his trousers, and the sound engineer (you know, the fella who sticks cords and microphones up your blouse!).

Then there is the wardrobe lady, the lovely Maria, and finally the make-up artist, Tina, who is literally in your face the second you walk onto the set every day. Thankfully, Tina is very good at her job, being extremely professional and, most importantly, very sensitive to one's space and privacy. She needs to be: I hate wearing layers of make-up – it just isn't me!

'Just look to the left, Kylie,' she says, 'I am applying the liquid eyeliner now.' You can't imagine how strange this feels. It's as if a small snail is sliming across your very sensitive eyelid. I feel claustrophobic, like a caged animal – I never normally sit still for this long!

'Don't worry, Kyles!' Simon, the director, bellows from across the room. 'Just relax! Tina knows what she's doing, darling – and through the camera lens, it will look very natural.'

'How will 14 layers of foundation look natural?' I mutter under my breath.

Meanwhile, I'm still plotting ways to scrape and claw this thick stuff off my face . . .

sautéed chicken livers served with watercress and radish salad

I particularly enjoy chicken livers prepared in a French or Italian fashion. I adore the depth and intoxicating flavour of the reduced brandy, and I use French butter for authenticity. The sweetness of the sugar in this recipe is complemented by the sour yet soft flavour of the sherry vinegar – it is interesting to note that many chicken liver dishes, no matter what cuisine they represent, are teamed with sweet and sour flavours. I believe chicken livers should only ever be served rare, so they retain their silky, rich, delicate texture and flavour.

Trim and wash chicken livers, pat dry with kitchen paper and set aside.

Heat oil in a heavy-based frying pan, add shallots and salt and stir over high heat for 1 minute. Add sugar and cook, stirring, for about 2 minutes, or until shallots are lightly browned. Reduce heat, add water and simmer for 1 minute to caramelise shallots further. Remove shallots from the pan with a slotted spoon and set aside.

Add half the butter to pan and simmer until melted and bubbling, then add half the chicken livers. Fry over high heat very briefly on both sides, so they are lightly browned but still pink in the middle (it is better to undercook the livers at this point). Remove from pan and cover with foil. Repeat with the other half of the butter and chicken livers.

Add brandy and vinegar to the pan juices and simmer for about 5 minutes, or until liquid is reduced by half. Return chicken livers to the pan, along with the extra salt and the caramelised shallots, and stir over high heat for 30 seconds, or until just heated through.

Finally, combine salad ingredients in a bowl and toss gently.

To serve, arrange the sautéed livers on a platter and top with the salad. Sprinkle with pepper, and serve with toasted sourdough bread.

Serve as a starter for 4–6

500 g (1 lb) organic chicken livers

2 tablespoons olive oil

4 golden shallots, peeled and crushed

1 teaspoon sea salt

2 tablespoons white sugar

1 tablespoon water

90 g (3 oz) French butter

$\frac{1}{2}$ cup brandy

$\frac{1}{2}$ cup sherry vinegar

$\frac{1}{2}$ teaspoon sea salt, extra

pinch cracked white pepper

toasted sourdough bread, to serve

WATERCRESS AND RADISH SALAD

$1\frac{1}{3}$ cups watercress sprigs

$\frac{1}{3}$ cup finely sliced red radishes

1 tablespoon lemon juice

1 tablespoon extra virgin olive oil

$\frac{1}{2}$ teaspoon sea salt

slow-cooked honeycomb tripe with fresh green peas

Honeycomb tripe is a real favourite of mine, even though it looks rather like a bathing cap with its crazy patterning! This recipe was inspired by my short but delightful stint at The Restaurant Manfredi, where Franca and Stefano Manfredi cooked the most delicious tripe à la Milanese. I've added green apples, for sourness, and bacon bones (ask your butcher to saw them into slices), for their smokiness. Serve this with crusty sourdough bread to mop up the sauce.

Bring water and vinegar to the boil in a large pan. Reduce heat, add tripe and simmer gently, covered, for 30 minutes. Drain tripe, refresh under cold water, drain again and slice finely.

Meanwhile, using a mortar and pestle, gently press tomatoes until they are slightly bruised and have released their juices; transfer to a bowl and set aside. Add garlic and half the salt to the mortar and pestle and pound into a rough paste. Set aside.

Place sugar and water in a medium-sized frying pan and stir over low heat, without boiling, until sugar is dissolved. Bring to the boil, then simmer, uncovered, without stirring, for about 3 minutes, or until mixture turns light caramel in colour. (The caramel is ready when a spoonful dropped into a cup of cold water can be moulded into a soft ball with the fingers.)

Heat oil in a heavy-based frying pan, add reserved garlic paste and sauté for 1 minute, or until aromatic. Stir in fennel, onions, celery, bacon bones and remaining salt, and cook, stirring occasionally, for about 2 minutes. Add tripe and stir to combine. Pour in caramel mixture and tomatoes and stir well to coat tripe in the caramel. Add wine and chardonnay vinegar and simmer, uncovered, for about 10 minutes, or until liquid is reduced by half. Pour in stock, cover pan and simmer gently for 25 minutes. Stir in apples and cook, covered, for a further 25 minutes, or until the tripe is tender.

Remove the lid, stir in peas and simmer, uncovered, for about 6 minutes, or until peas are just tender. Remove from stove and stir in remaining ingredients.

Serve as a main meal for 4–6

3 litres (3 quarts) water

½ cup white wine vinegar

1 kg (2 lb) honeycomb tripe, roughly sliced

5 small roma (plum) tomatoes, cut into quarters

10 garlic cloves

2 teaspoons sea salt

⅔ cup palm sugar

⅓ cup water

1 cup extra virgin olive oil

1 small baby fennel bulb, finely sliced

12 small salad onions, trimmed, but with 2 cm (1 in) green stem left intact

1 small stick of celery, sliced on the diagonal

200 g (6½ oz) smoked bacon bones, sliced

1 cup white wine

⅓ cup chardonnay vinegar

3 cups chicken stock (page 187)

4 small green apples, peeled and roughly chopped

1 cup shelled peas – about 500 g (1 lb) fresh peas in their pods

2–3 teaspoons salt, extra

1 tablespoon red wine vinegar

1 tablespoon chardonnay vinegar, extra

red-braised beef oxtail with roast tomatoes and garlic

Serve as part of a banquet for 6

1 kg (2 lb) beef oxtail

1 quantity red-braising stock (page 192)

3 garlic bulbs, unpeeled

$\frac{1}{2}$ cup extra virgin olive oil

4 medium-sized vine-ripened tomatoes

$\frac{1}{4}$ bunch tarragon

1 teaspoon sea salt

pinch cracked white pepper

1 tablespoon sherry vinegar

1 tablespoon red wine vinegar

1 tablespoon chardonnay vinegar

I love red-braising cheaper cuts of meat, like oxtail and brisket, because of their ability to absorb flavours and aromatics – can you imagine the intensity of flavour that is instilled into the meat over several hours of slow braising? When you bite into the melt-in-your-mouth meat, you get this immediate burst of ginger, star anise, cassia bark, soy sauce, garlic, a beautiful mellowness from the shao hsing wine, and that unmistakeable scent of sesame oil.

Place oxtail in a large pan, cover with cold water and bring to the boil. Simmer for 20 minutes, then drain, discarding the water. Rinse oxtail thoroughly under cold water and drain well. (This process rids the meat of any impurities prior to braising.)

In a large stockpot, bring red-braising stock to the boil. Transfer oxtail to simmering stock, ensuring it is fully submerged. Braise very gently for 2–3 hours, or until oxtail is soft and gelatinous, skimming stock regularly with a ladle. Remove pot from stove and set aside.

Meanwhile, roast garlic and tomatoes separately. Place garlic bulbs in a roasting tin and drizzle with 1 tablespoon of the olive oil. Cover with foil and roast at 150°C (300°F) for about $1\frac{1}{2}$ hours, or until very soft and slightly caramelised. Place tomatoes in another roasting tin, drizzle with remaining olive oil, and sprinkle with tarragon leaves, salt and pepper. Roast at 150°C (300°F) for about 1 hour, or until very soft and slightly collapsed.

Allow garlic to cool slightly, then cut bulbs in half crossways and squeeze pulp into a bowl. Combine pulp with 2 teaspoons of the red-braising stock.

Remove tomatoes from tin and reserve. Pour tomato pan juices into a bowl and combine with the vinegars to make a dressing.

Using tongs, gently remove oxtail from stock and arrange on a large platter. Top with reserved tomatoes, drizzle with the vinegar dressing and garnish with a spoonful of roasted garlic.

luscious bacon braised with red wine and fresh cherries

Although braised bacon is traditionally a rather frugal meal, I've made it luscious by using the finest organic bacon and adding red wine and cherries. With its beautiful pink meat and a rich, deep-red sauce, this dish is ideal for Christmas or any other celebration. The rind is best left on the bacon during cooking, to keep the meat moist and succulent, but you can remove it before slicing and serving, if you prefer. Dried sour cherries and quince paste are available from good delicatessens.

Combine all ingredients except bacon in a large bowl. Add bacon and toss well to coat in the marinade. Cover and refrigerate for 3–4 hours.

Preheat oven to 200°C (400°F). Transfer bacon to a roasting tin and pour over the marinade. Bake, covered with foil, for 35 minutes, then remove foil and bake for a further 20 minutes, or until bacon is cooked through.

Slice bacon, arrange on a platter and spoon over the cherries, bay leaves and pan juices.

Serve as a main meal for 6

1 cup red wine

1 cup fresh cherries

½ cup dried sour cherries

2 tablespoons raw sugar

1 teaspoon salt

2 tablespoons extra virgin olive oil

4 garlic cloves, crushed

½ cup sherry vinegar

2 tablespoons quince paste

6 bay leaves

1 × 750 g (1½ lb) piece fresh, organic bacon with rind

roast cinnamon chicken with lemon and cider vinegar dressing

Serve as a main meal for 4

1 × 1.5 kg (3 lb) free-range chicken

2 lemons, thickly sliced

8 bay leaves

PEPPERBERRY BUTTER

2 teaspoons dried native Australian
pepperberries or whole black peppercorns

3 garlic cloves

4 cm (1½ in) knob ginger, sliced

1 teaspoon sea salt

½ teaspoon ground cinnamon

1 teaspoon ground cumin

125 g (4 oz) unsalted butter

LEMON AND CIDER VINEGAR DRESSING

1 small lemon

1 garlic clove, finely diced

2 teaspoons sea salt

½ cup extra virgin olive oil

¼ cup lemon juice

1 tablespoon cider vinegar

2 salad onions, finely sliced

2 teaspoons finely grated lemon zest

I love the spicy, tingly flavour of pepperberries, which are available in selected delicatessens. Their pepperiness is perfectly offset by the delicious sourness of fresh lemons.

To make the pepperberry butter, pound pepperberries, garlic, ginger, salt and ground spices with a pestle and mortar until well crushed. Mix in the butter until well combined. Set aside.

Rinse chicken under cold water. Trim away excess fat from inside and outside cavity, but keep neck, parson's nose and winglets intact. Tuck wing tips under chicken, then place in a lightly oiled roasting tin, breast-side up. Using your hands, ease the breast and thigh skin away from the meat, being careful not to tear the skin. Place half of the reserved butter mixture between the skin and meat of the chicken, spreading it evenly under the skin. Make a couple of cuts in thigh meat to help the heat and flavours to penetrate more easily. Rub remaining butter over outside of chicken. Place lemons and bay leaves inside cavity. Cover and refrigerate for 1 hour.

Preheat oven to 190°C (375°F). Roast chicken, uncovered, for about 1 hour, or until juices run clear and skin is crisp and lightly browned. Remove from oven, cover with foil and leave in a warm place for 10 minutes.

Meanwhile, make the dressing. Cut a slice from one end of the lemon and stand the lemon cut-side down on a chopping board. Using a small, sharp knife, cut the skin and pith away, slicing from top to bottom and following the curve of the fruit. Cut the flesh into segments by slicing between the membranes of each section to the centre of the lemon. Pound garlic and salt with a pestle and mortar until you have a rough paste. Mix in the lemon segments and bruise slightly to release juices. Add remaining ingredients, mix well and set aside.

Remove chicken from tin, reserving pan juices. Slice chicken and arrange on a platter with lemon slices and bay leaves, drizzling with pan juices. Serve dressing in a bowl on the side.

red-braised brisket with caramelised shallots and fresh chilli

Serve as part of a banquet for 6

This is a very lovely recipe to cook – I just adore watching sugar do its caramelising thing in a good, heavy pan; the moment when the sugar turns that warm, honey-caramel colour is magical. The final dish is rather complex: in addition to the myriad flavours of red-braising stock, the tomato salad is fresh, sour, salty and sweet all at once, and the onions are sweet, sticky, aniseedy, vinegary and simply delectable! Imagine the experience of tasting all this at once. And don't forget, there will be a little kick of chilli in there, too . . .

1 kg (2 lb) brisket, cut into 5 cm (2 in) thick slices

1 quantity red-braising stock (page 192)

2 medium-sized vine-ripened tomatoes

½ teaspoon white sugar

1½ tablespoons lime juice

1 teaspoon sea salt

6 small, perfect iceberg lettuce leaves

pinch Sichuan pepper

1 large red chilli, finely sliced

CARAMELISED SHALLOTS

2½ tablespoons peanut oil

2 salad onions, trimmed and finely sliced

6 cm (2½ in) knob ginger, sliced

4 garlic cloves, crushed

1 teaspoon sea salt

250 g (8 oz) red shallots, peeled

¼ cup shao hsing wine

4 tablespoons crushed yellow rock sugar

⅓ cup chicken stock (page 187)

2 tablespoons mushroom soy sauce

3 whole star anise

Place brisket in a large pan, cover with cold water and bring to the boil. Simmer for 20 minutes, then drain, discarding the water. Rinse brisket thoroughly under cold water and drain well. (This process rids the meat of any impurities prior to braising.)

In a large stockpot, bring red-braising stock to the boil. Transfer brisket to simmering stock, ensuring it is fully submerged. Braise very gently for 2 hours, or until brisket is soft and gelatinous, skimming stock regularly with a ladle. Remove pot from stove and set aside.

Meanwhile, cut tomatoes into wedges and combine in a bowl with sugar, lime juice and salt. Refrigerate for 30 minutes.

Next, make the caramelised shallots. Heat peanut oil in a heavy-based frying pan and add onions, ginger, garlic and salt. Cook, stirring, for about 2 minutes, or until lightly browned. Add shallots and cook over low heat for a further 5 minutes, stirring constantly. Increase heat, add wine and simmer for 1 minute to deglaze the pan. Add remaining ingredients and simmer gently, uncovered, for about 20 minutes, or until shallots are very tender and caramelised.

Finally, using tongs, remove brisket from the stock and slice. Arrange lettuce leaves on a large platter and top with brisket. Drizzle with some of the hot stock and sprinkle with Sichuan pepper. Serve with the caramelised shallots, tomato salad and fresh chilli.

braised quails with fresh figs and green grapes

This beautiful combination of quail and grapes was inspired by Claudia Roden's book *The Food of Italy*. I've added fresh figs because I just love their flavour and texture. With the meatiness of quail, the softness of figs and the crunchiness of grapes, this dish is all about texture. Although it's an inexpensive dish to make, the overall effect is very exotic. The addition of wine and vinegar towards the end of the cooking time, and the butter melted in at the last minute, produces a rich sauce with just the right amount of piquancy – perfect for mopping up with bread. Of course, the only way to really get to grips with the quails themselves is with your fingers!

Pound garlic, ginger and half the salt with a pestle and mortar until you have a coarse paste.

Wash grapes well, remove from stem and set aside.

Wash quails and pat dry with kitchen paper. Tie the legs together with kitchen string so quails retain their shape. Season with pepper and remaining salt.

Heat olive oil in a large frying pan and seal quails on all sides over high heat until lightly browned. Reduce heat, allow oil to cool for about 1 minute, then stir in garlic and ginger paste. Cook, stirring occasionally, for about 4 minutes, or until the garlic is very soft and aromatic. Increase heat, then add figs, grapes and olives, and cook for about 3 minutes to sear the fruit. Pour in wine and vinegar, bring to the boil and then simmer for a further 3 minutes, or until the liquid has reduced slightly. Reduce heat, scatter butter over quails and braise very gently, covered, for about 15 minutes, or until quails are just cooked through. Do not allow the dish to return to the boil, otherwise the sauce will separate.

Remove quails from pan, discard string and arrange on a platter. Spoon over fruit, olives and all the pan juices.

Serve as a main meal for 4–6

5 garlic cloves, peeled

4 cm (1½ in) knob ginger, sliced

2 teaspoons sea salt

300 g (10 oz) bunch seedless green grapes

6 × 200 g (6½ oz) quails

pinch cracked white pepper

½ cup extra virgin olive oil

7 small fresh figs, cut in half

100 g (3½ oz) small green olives, pitted

½ cup white wine

¼ cup chardonnay vinegar

100 g (3½ oz) unsalted butter, chopped

french-style brisket salad

Serve as part of a banquet for 4–6

1.25 kg (2½ lb) brisket, cut into 5 cm (2 in) thick slices

STOCK

4 litres (4 quarts) water

2 cups white wine

3 salad onions, trimmed and sliced

1 small leek, sliced

10 cm (4 in) knob ginger, sliced

12 garlic cloves, crushed

½ bunch flat-leaf parsley, cut in half crossways

¼ cup sea salt

1 tablespoon white sugar

1 tablespoon white peppercorns

8 bay leaves

SALAD

1 medium-sized cucumber, peeled

1 tablespoon chardonnay vinegar

1 teaspoon sea salt

1 teaspoon white sugar

1 tablespoon salted capers, rinsed and drained

1 small red onion, finely diced

1 cup diced ox-heart (beef) tomatoes

1 tablespoon Dijon mustard

1 teaspoon sea salt, extra

⅓ cup extra virgin olive oil

1 tablespoon chardonnay vinegar, extra

2 tablespoons chervil leaves

2 tablespoons roughly chopped flat-leaf parsley

2 tablespoons roughly chopped tarragon

This is my spin on an old French recipe. It is important to leave the fat on the brisket during cooking so that the meat remains moist and tender. If you like, you can trim some of the excess fat after braising.

Place brisket in a large pan, cover with cold water and bring to the boil. Simmer for 20 minutes, then strain through a colander, discarding the water. Rinse brisket thoroughly under cold water and drain well. (This process rids the meat of any impurities prior to braising.)

Place all stock ingredients in a 10-litre (10-quart) stockpot and bring to the boil. Transfer brisket to simmering stock, ensuring it is fully submerged. Reduce heat and simmer gently, covered, for about 2½ hours, or until brisket is soft and gelatinous. Skim stock regularly, using a ladle. Remove brisket from stock and set aside to cool; trim off some of the fat, if desired.

For the salad, cut cucumber in half lengthways and scoop out seeds. Using a mandoline or a very sharp knife, finely slice into 10 cm (4 in) ribbons and place in a bowl with vinegar, salt and sugar. Cover and refrigerate for 1 hour.

To serve, combine chilled cucumber with remaining salad ingredients. Slice reserved brisket and arrange on a platter with the salad.

roast red onions filled with veal, tarragon and olives

This dish is hearty and comforting. I particularly love the salty olives mixed with sweet dates in the filling, and the garnish of roasted hazelnuts adds a wonderful crunch and nuttiness. It is important not to overcook the onions initially, or they will not hold their shape when filled and roasted.

Bring a large pan of water to the boil, add onions, reduce heat and simmer, uncovered, for about 20 minutes, or until onions are almost tender. Drain and set aside to cool.

Preheat oven to 160°C (325°F).

To make the filling, take handfuls of the veal and throw them hard against the side of a large bowl to tenderise the meat. Combine with all remaining filling ingredients.

When onions have cooled, cut in half crossways and discard centres, leaving a shell of the outer two layers (don't worry if there's a hole at the base of the onion, as it will be covered by the filling). Divide filling between onion cups and place filled onions in a roasting tin. Pour wine into tin, drizzle onions with half the oil and cover tin with foil. Bake for 10 minutes, then remove foil and bake for a further 10 minutes, or until just cooked through.

While the onions are roasting, make the sauce. Place sliced onions in a small, heavy-based pan. Add garlic and salt and top with tomatoes. Pour over the oil and place pan over high heat for about 3 minutes, or until mixture comes to the boil. Reduce heat and simmer gently, uncovered, for about 25 minutes, or until sauce has reduced by half. Stir in preserved lemon rind and chilli and remove from the stove.

Arrange onions on a platter, spoon over the sauce, then garnish with hazelnuts and drizzle over a little extra virgin olive oil.

Serve as a light meal for 4,
or as part of a banquet for 4–6

4 × 200 g (6½ oz) red onions, peeled

¼ cup white wine

2 tablespoons extra virgin olive oil

¼ cup roasted hazelnuts, coarsely chopped

FILLING

300 g (10 oz) organic veal mince (ground veal)

⅓ cup small pitted green olives, chopped

2 fresh dates, seeded and chopped

4 garlic cloves, finely diced

1½ tablespoons roughly chopped tarragon

⅓ cup roughly chopped chervil

⅓ cup roughly chopped flat-leaf parsley

60 g (2 oz) semi-dried tomatoes, chopped

¼ cup extra virgin olive oil

1 egg

1 teaspoon sea salt

small pinch cracked white pepper

FRESH TOMATO SAUCE

½ cup finely sliced salad onions

2 garlic cloves, roughly chopped

1 teaspoon sea salt

350 g (11 oz) ox-heart (beef) tomatoes, roughly diced

2 tablespoons extra virgin olive oil

1 teaspoon finely diced preserved lemon rind

½ large red chilli, deseeded and finely sliced on the diagonal

moroccan-style meatballs served with sour cherry and date sauce

Claudia Roden's book *Tamarind and Saffron* opened my eyes to the wonderful and enticing world of Middle Eastern and North African cuisine. I love the use of exotic spices and herbs – there's a romanticism and an alluring quality to this style of cooking that's intriguingly different to the Chinese flavours I am used too. These meatballs are very rich, but the richness is balanced by the sourness of the sauce. This is a joyous recipe to prepare, intensive yet worth it!

Preheat oven to 200°C (400°F). Place capsicums in a roasting tin and drizzle with olive oil. Roast, uncovered, for about 35 minutes, or until skin blisters and blackens, turning once halfway through cooking time. Transfer capsicums and pan juices to a bowl, cover with plastic wrap and leave to stand for 10 minutes. Drain off juices for later use. Peel skin from capsicums, cut in half and remove seeds and membranes. Roughly chop flesh and set aside.

Pound garlic, ginger and salt with a pestle and mortar until you have a fine paste. Combine pork and beef mince, then take handfuls of the mixture and throw them hard against the side of a large bowl to tenderise the meat. Add reserved capsicum, garlic and ginger paste, eggs and all remaining meatball ingredients. Combine well, using your hands. >

Serve as a main meal for 6
(makes about 30 meatballs)

MEATBALLS

2 large red capsicums (bell peppers)

5 tablespoons extra virgin olive oil

8 garlic cloves

4 tablespoons roughly chopped ginger

1 tablespoon sea salt

500 g (1 lb) pork mince (ground pork)

500 g (1 lb) beef mince (ground beef)

2 eggs

½ cup extra virgin olive oil, extra

2 medium-sized red onions, finely diced

5 tablespoons diced mustard fruits

2 tablespoons finely diced fresh turmeric

1 tablespoon diced preserved lemon rind

½ cup roughly chopped coriander leaves

⅓ cup finely sliced coriander stems and roots

⅓ cup roughly chopped mint

⅓ cup roughly chopped flat-leaf parsley

2 tablespoons honey

2 tablespoons balsamic vinegar

2 teaspoons ground cumin

1½ teaspoons ground cinnamon

pinch cracked white pepper

about ½ cup plain (all-purpose) flour

olive oil

SOUR CHERRY AND DATE SAUCE

¼ cup dried blueberries

¼ cup dried cranberries

¼ cup extra virgin olive oil

5 salad onions, trimmed and finely sliced

3 teaspoons sea salt

¾ cup dried sour cherries

4 fresh dates, sliced

6 bay leaves

1 tablespoon sherry vinegar

1 tablespoon plain Greek-style yoghurt

Shape ¼ cups of the meatball mixture into balls, then toss in flour to lightly coat. Heat oil in a large frying pan and shallow-fry meatballs in batches until lightly browned and cooked through. Drain well on kitchen paper and keep warm.

Meanwhile, for the sauce, soak blueberries and cranberries in ¾ cup of boiling water for 20 minutes. Strain, reserving the soaking water as well as the fruit. Heat oil in a medium-sized frying pan. Add onions and salt, and cook, stirring, for about 3 minutes, or until onions are soft. Add cherries and cook, stirring, for a further 2 minutes. Stir in dates, bay leaves, berries with their soaking water and ½ cup of the reserved capsicum-pan juices. Simmer, uncovered, for about 5 minutes, or until fruit has softened and mixture is slightly reduced. Stir in vinegar.

To serve, place the meatballs in a shallow bowl, spoon over the sour cherry sauce and top with a generous dollop of yoghurt.

糖水荔枝

FRUCHTKONSERVE
elgewicht 227 g.

LYCHEES OP WATER, LICHT GEZCET
NETTO INHOUD 567 GRAM
NET WT 1–LB. 4–OZS. (567 GRAM

ORTE DE LA R. P. DE CHINE

Western and Eastern

At the ABC's Gore Hill studios a set has been built especially for this TV show, so it looks as if I'm in my home – in my kitchen or my hallway, my dining room or my study/thinking area. The way the set evolved was wonderful: Simon, the director, and Samantha Paxton, the set designer, spent lots of time talking with me. We visited shops and flicked through piles of magazines and books. Next, I created a scrapbook, a sort of visual journal, to capture the essence of my home and what I love to furnish it with. Starting with a lovely, big, black leather-bound book with white pages, I pasted in all my favourite things: paintings; poetry; rich fabrics in earthy tones of burgundy, dark brown, dark green and burnt orange, as well as brilliant, quirky hues of cobalt and magenta; pictures of chandeliers and beautiful candles cut out of my treasured architecture and interior-design magazines.

I guess you could describe the final style as rustic – textured and layered, warm and rich. I wanted something soulful and a little bit crazy . . . like a chandelier hanging in the boudoir. I always wanted a chandelier, and one day I just said, 'We must have a chandelier! We must have a chandelier! If there's anything I want it's a chandelier, because not only is it opulent and beautiful and delicate, but it's also a little bit mad.'

The way my house looks is very important to me – it's like my sanctuary. I treat my home as my sacred space, so I'm particular about what I put in my house and where. Fortunately Samantha and Simon understood this; they allowed room for it to breathe and created this wonderful, inspiring set where I feel completely comfortable. I love being there and I love cooking in it. I especially love the mood lighting, and I love entertaining people there.

king prawn and chilli salad
with soft-boiled duck eggs

As an apprentice chef at Rockpool, I asked Neil Perry, my head chef and employer, where he received his inspiration from, where he had learnt to cook. He simply replied, 'Kwongy, just read all of Elizabeth David's cookbooks and you will learn everything that a cook needs to know!'

When the doyenne of English food writing was crafting the recipes that were to change the eating habits of generations, dressing prawns with chilli and olive oil would have been considered quite risqué. This, then, is my tribute to Elizabeth David's spirit of adventure – and to the humble prawn cocktail. I've always loved the delicious combination of prawns and iceberg lettuce, but my version has a touch of chilli zing and the richness of duck eggs. Hen eggs may be substituted for the duck eggs, just as long as they are fresh; for soft-boiled hen eggs, reduce the boiling time to 4 minutes.

Bring a small pan of water to the boil, add eggs and boil for 7 minutes. Drain, refresh in cold water and peel. Reserve for later use.

Add prawns to a large pan of boiling salted water and boil for 1 minute. Drain, refresh in iced water and drain immediately. Peel and devein the prawns, cutting them in half on the diagonal. Set aside.

To make the paste, pound chillies, ginger, garlic, oil and salt with a pestle and mortar until you have a coarse paste. Stir in reserved prawns, lime juice and lemon juice.

Divide lettuce between individual bowls and top with prawn salad. Cut the reserved eggs in half and garnish each salad with half an egg. Sprinkle with salt and pepper.

Serve as a starter for 4

2 free-range duck eggs

12 uncooked king prawns (jumbo shrimp)

¼ iceberg lettuce, very finely shredded

pinch sea salt

pinch cracked white pepper

PASTE

1 large red chilli, deseeded and roughly chopped

1 large green chilli, deseeded and roughly chopped

4 cm (1½ in) knob ginger, sliced

2 garlic cloves

⅓ cup extra virgin olive oil

1¼ teaspoons sea salt

1 tablespoon lime juice

1 tablespoon lemon juice

crunchy and runny duck eggs topped with scallops and chervil

Serve as a starter for 4

1½ cups vegetable oil

4 free-range duck eggs

2 tablespoons extra virgin olive oil

16 sea scallops, removed from the shell

⅓ cup diced ox-heart (beef) tomatoes

2 tablespoons chervil leaves

1 teaspoon balsamic vinegar

pinch sea salt

pinch cracked white pepper

This recipe is a celebration of fresh duck eggs. I just love them when they're fried like this, so they're crunchy on the bottom but soft and gooey in the middle. If you can't find duck eggs, hen eggs are fine – as long as they're very fresh. Because this dish has so few ingredients, they must all be absolutely fresh and of the best quality. Juicy tomatoes, chervil and scallops are a match made in heaven.

Heat vegetable oil in a hot wok until the surface seems to shimmer slightly. Crack eggs into a small bowl, then pour into the hot oil. After 2 minutes, reduce heat to moderate to allow underside of eggs to become firm (the yolks should still be runny at this point).

Carefully slide a fish slice under eggs and lift out of wok, then pour off the oil. Return eggs to wok and put back over the heat for another 2 minutes to crisp further. Gently remove eggs from wok and drain off any excess oil before easing onto a warm plate.

Add 1 tablespoon of olive oil to wok and add scallops. Sear for about 1 minute on each side, or until lightly browned and just cooked through.

Scatter tomatoes over eggs and garnish with scallops and chervil. Drizzle with vinegar and remaining oil, and sprinkle with salt and pepper. Serve immediately.

kylie's 'radical' roast chicken

Everyone has a favourite roast chicken recipe, and this is mine –
a slightly radical version of the classic roast chook, using Chinese
double-cooking techniques for a juicy chicken with maximum flavour.
The chicken is first 'steamed' in the oven under foil, so it doesn't dry
out, then the foil is removed and the heat turned up to give it a lovely
crispy skin.

Preheat oven to 220°C (450°F). Rinse chicken under cold
water. Trim away excess fat from inside and outside cavity, but
keep neck, parson's nose and winglets intact. Tuck wing tips
under chicken. Place chicken in roasting tin, breast-side up.

Place tarragon and half the rosemary inside cavity of chicken.
Using your hands, carefully separate the skin from the meat
over the breast and thighs of the chicken. Place the butter
between the skin and the meat, spreading it evenly under
the skin.

Lightly crush unpeeled garlic cloves and scatter over chicken
with bay leaves, salt and remaining rosemary.

Place carrots, sweet potatoes, potatoes and shallots around
chicken, then drizzle with oil and sprinkle with pepper.

Cover roasting tin with foil and roast for 35 minutes. Remove
from oven and reduce temperature to 180°C (350°F). Take off
foil and bake for a further 20 minutes, or until chicken is just
cooked through and vegetables are tender. To test chicken,
insert a skewer into the thigh and press against the meat –
it is cooked when the juices run clear. The skin should be
crisp and lightly browned. Remove chicken from oven, cover
with foil and leave to rest in a warm place for 10 minutes.

Remove chicken from tin and serve with the roast vegetables
and some crusty sourdough bread.

Serve as a main meal for 4–6

1 × 1.5 kg (3 lb) free-range chicken

½ bunch tarragon

4 sprigs rosemary, roughly chopped

100 g (3½ oz) unsalted butter, sliced

1 whole garlic bulb

10 bay leaves

1 tablespoon sea salt

2 medium-sized carrots, peeled
and cut into wedges

2 small sweet potatoes, peeled
and cut into wedges

6 medium-sized kipfler potatoes,
peeled and cut into wedges

5 small golden shallots, unpeeled
but cut in half

⅓ cup extra virgin olive oil

pinch cracked white pepper

sourdough bread, to serve

roast stuffed shoulder of lamb with apricot and chestnut sauce

This is a beautifully warming and generous dish. You can buy glacé apricots and whole peeled chestnuts from selected delicatessens. The apricots are usually kept in large glass jars – ask for the amount you need – and the chestnuts are sold in cans or vacuum-sealed packs. Serve the lamb with toasted sourdough bread and a freshly tossed leaf salad.

Preheat oven to 180°C (350°F).

For the stuffing, heat butter and oil in small frying pan and cook onions, stirring, for about 3 minutes, or until onion is soft. Transfer to a bowl, add all remaining stuffing ingredients and mix well.

Lay lamb skin-side down on a chopping board. Spread stuffing evenly over lamb, roll tightly to enclose stuffing and secure with kitchen string at 2 cm (1 in) intervals. Rub lamb with a little salt and pepper. Heat oil in a medium-sized frying pan and seal lamb over high heat until lightly browned all over. Transfer to a roasting tin and bake, uncovered, for about 35 minutes, or until cooked as desired. Remove from oven, cover with foil and leave to rest in a warm place for 10 minutes. Reserve pan juices for later use.

While lamb is resting, make the sauce. Pour ³/₄ cup of reserved pan juices into a large frying pan and bring to the boil. Reduce heat to medium, stir in sugar and simmer, stirring, until sugar dissolves. Add vinegars, apricots and chestnuts and simmer, stirring occasionally, for about 5 minutes, or until mixture caramelises slightly. Remove from stove and stir in lemon juice and salt.

Remove string from lamb and slice thickly. Arrange on a platter and spoon over the apricot and chestnut sauce.

Serve as a main meal for 6

1.75 kg (3½ lb) lamb shoulder, boned

pinch sea salt

pinch cracked white pepper

¼ cup extra virgin olive oil

APRICOT, ALMOND AND MUSHROOM STUFFING

50 g (1½ oz) unsalted butter

1 tablespoon extra virgin olive oil

1 cup finely diced brown onion

⅓ cup glacé apricots

⅓ cup smoked almonds, roughly crushed

100 g (3½ oz) shiitake mushrooms, stems removed and finely sliced

⅓ cup finely chopped mint

⅓ cup finely chopped flat-leaf parsley

2 tablespoons finely chopped tarragon

2 tablespoons finely chopped chervil

1 teaspoon finely grated orange zest

1 tablespoon sea salt

APRICOT AND CHESTNUT SAUCE

¼ cup raw sugar

¼ cup red wine vinegar

¼ cup sherry vinegar

6 fresh apricots, halved

150 g (5 oz) peeled whole chestnuts

½ tablespoon lemon juice

1 teaspoon sea salt

deep-fried fillets of snapper served with lively tomato salad

This is my take on traditional beer-battered fish, given extra zest by a citrussy tomato salad. The success of this recipe depends entirely on obtaining the freshest fish. Other suitable fish are King George whiting, flathead, gurnard, garfish and sand whiting.

Combine batter ingredients in a bowl with a slotted spoon. (Using a spoon rather than a whisk keeps the batter thick and lumpy, and the lumps become crunchy when deep-fried). Leave the batter at room temperature until the ice has melted, then use immediately.

Meanwhile, make the tomato salad. Pound salt and peppercorns with a pestle and mortar until roughly ground. Add vine-ripened and ox-heart tomatoes and lightly crush. Pour in olive oil, lemon and lime juices and mix well. Stir in pear tomatoes and green tomato and transfer salad to a bowl. Cover and refrigerate until ready to use.

Lightly toss fish fillets in flour, then dip in batter to coat completely, letting any excess drain off. Heat vegetable oil in a large frying pan until the surface seems to shimmer slightly, then add fish in batches and fry for about 3 minutes, or until lightly browned. Remove fish from oil and drain on kitchen paper.

Arrange fish on a large platter and serve with tomato salad on the side.

Serve as part of a banquet for 6

6 × 100 g (3½ oz) snapper fillets

¼ cup plain (all-purpose) flour

2 cups vegetable oil for deep-frying

BEER BATTER

½ cup beer

½ cup plain (all-purpose) flour

½ cup ice

TOMATO SALAD

2 teaspoons sea salt

1 teaspoon white peppercorns

1 small vine-ripened tomato, roughly chopped

1 small ox-heart (beef) tomato, roughly chopped

2 tablespoons extra virgin olive oil

2 tablespoons lemon juice

2 teaspoons lime juice

10 yellow pear tomatoes, halved

1 small green tomato, roughly sliced

pigeon with peaches and witlof

Serve as a main meal for 2

1 × 500 g (1 lb) pigeon (squab)

1 quantity white-poaching stock (page 195)

2 witlof (Belgian endive)

2 tablespoons butter

¼ cup extra virgin olive oil

½ teaspoon sea salt

about 3 cups chicken stock (page 187)

pinch Sichuan pepper and salt (page 194)

CARAMELISED PEACHES

2 fresh peaches, preferably freestone variety

2 tablespoons palm sugar

2 tablespoons fish sauce

2 tablespoons lime juice

You could also use two quails for this recipe – just poach for 7 minutes.

Rinse pigeon under cold water, then trim away excess fat from inside and outside the cavity. Keep neck, parson's nose and winglets intact, but remove wingtips and claws. In a large stockpot, bring white-poaching stock to the boil. Lower pigeon, breast-side down, into simmering stock, ensuring it is fully submerged. Poach very gently for exactly 9 minutes. Remove pot from stove and allow pigeon to steep in stock for 2 hours at room temperature to complete the poaching process. Using tongs, gently remove pigeon from stock and place breast-side up on a wire rack over a tray to drain and cool.

Meanwhile, carefully cut the witlof almost completely in half lengthways but leave attached at the base. Heat butter and half the oil in a medium-sized frying pan, add witlof and sauté over medium heat for about 5 minutes, or until lightly browned. Add salt and enough stock to cover, then simmer, covered, for about 7 minutes, or until just tender. Remove from pan and set aside.

To make the caramelised peaches, cut a shallow cross in the bottom of each peach and drop into a pan of boiling water. Blanch for 10 seconds, remove with a slotted spoon and refresh under cold water. Carefully peel away skin, cut peaches in half and discard stones. Heat palm sugar and fish sauce in a heavy-based frying pan and simmer for about 2 minutes, or until syrupy and caramelised. Add peaches and simmer for a further 2 minutes. Remove pan from stove and stir in lime juice.

Preheat oven to 240°C (500°F). Heat remaining oil in a heavy-based frying pan and sear pigeon all over until golden brown. Transfer pigeon to a roasting tin and drizzle over the hot oil. Roast pigeon for 4 minutes. Remove pigeon from oven, cover with foil and leave in a warm place for 10 minutes. Remove head and neck of pigeon and discard. Remove wings, cut in half, and reserve for later. Place pigeon breast-side up on a chopping board and cut on either side of the breastbone to remove each half in one piece, then cut off the thighs and slice the breasts into 2 pieces on the diagonal. Arrange the pigeon and witlof on a platter and spoon over the caramelised peaches. Sprinkle with Sichuan pepper and salt and serve immediately.

kylie's wild lasagne

I just love making this lasagne! I revel in playing around with so many different ingredients, and there is nothing more satisfying than serving a slice of this lasagne and revealing all the many layers of deliciousness you have patiently created. Just remember that the tomatoes need to be very ripe and juicy, or you'll end up with a rather tame lasagne; and seek out some genuine Parmigiano-Reggiano – the long ageing process gives it a much more complex flavour. The lasagne can be put together several hours in advance, then just popped in the oven for an hour. Serve with some crusty bread and a freshly tossed salad.

Preheat oven to 150°C (300°F).

Trim base and most of green part from top of leeks, then cut in half lengthways. Rinse thoroughly to remove grit from between layers and cut into thirds crossways. Place leeks in a roasting tin, drizzle with oil and vinegar and sprinkle with salt and pepper. Cover tin tightly with foil and roast for about 35 minutes, or until leeks are tender. Remove from oven and increase the temperature to 180°C (350°F), ready for the lasagne.

Meanwhile, make the tomato sauce. Place onions in a medium-sized, heavy-based pan and top with finely sliced leek. Add garlic and salt to pan and lay tomatoes on top. Pour oil over tomatoes and place pan over high heat. Bring to the boil and simmer, uncovered, without stirring, for 8 minutes. Reduce heat and simmer gently, stirring occasionally, for a further 10 minutes, or until tomatoes begin to break down and the sauce thickens. Set aside. >

Serve as a main meal for 6–8

LEEKS

4 small leeks

⅔ cup extra virgin olive oil

¼ cup balsamic vinegar

2 teaspoons sea salt

pinch cracked white pepper

TOMATO SAUCE

2 medium-sized brown onions, cut in half and finely sliced

1 small leek, finely sliced

12 garlic cloves, crushed

1 tablespoon sea salt

2.25 kg (4½ lb) ox-heart (beef) tomatoes, roughly chopped

⅔ cup extra virgin olive oil

SILVER BEET

75 g (2½ oz) unsalted butter

6 garlic cloves, finely diced

1 teaspoon sea salt

1 bunch silver beet (Swiss chard),
stems discarded and leaves roughly chopped

¼ cup lemon juice

MUSHROOMS

50 g (1½ oz) unsalted butter, extra

180 g (6 oz) fresh shiitake mushrooms,
stems discarded and caps sliced

90 g (3 oz) fresh shimeji mushrooms,
stems discarded

2 tablespoons red wine vinegar

pinch sea salt

2 tablespoons olive oil

LASAGNE

375 g (12 oz) fresh lasagne – about 8 sheets

¼ cup roughly chopped mint

¼ cup roughly chopped flat-leaf parsley

750 g (1½ lb) fresh ricotta cheese

100 g (3½ oz) Reggiano parmesan, shaved

150 g (5 oz) small green olives,
pitted and halved

300 g (10 oz) fresh mozzarella cheese,
thinly sliced

dash of extra virgin olive oil

pinch cracked white pepper

Melt butter in a large, shallow frying pan, add garlic and salt, and cook gently for 2 minutes. Add silver beet and cook for a further 2 minutes, or until silver beet has just wilted. Add lemon juice and set aside to cool. Gently squeeze out excess liquid from the silver beet.

Melt extra butter in another frying pan; add mushrooms, vinegar and a pinch of salt. Cook, stirring occasionally, for about 2 minutes, or until mushrooms soften. Drain off any excess liquid.

To assemble the lasagne, brush a deep rectangular ovenproof dish – about 30 × 28 × 9 cm (12 × 11 × 3½ in) – with olive oil. Place a single layer of lasagne sheets in the dish. Cover with a quarter of the tomato sauce, followed by a third of the leeks and half the herbs. Scatter with half the ricotta and half the parmesan. Top with another layer of lasagne sheets, another quarter of the tomato sauce and all the olives. Scatter with half the silver beet, another third of the leeks and remaining ricotta. Add a third layer of lasagne sheets, another quarter of the tomato sauce, the mushrooms, remaining leeks, silver beet and herbs. Top with sliced mozzarella and a little shaved parmesan. Finally, cover with the last of the lasagne sheets and all except a couple of spoonfuls of the tomato sauce.

Bake, covered, for 50 minutes. Remove foil, increase oven temperature to 220°C (450°F) and bake for a further 10 minutes, or until lightly browned and cooked through.

Gently heat remaining tomato sauce, cut lasagne into generous pieces and serve on a plate with a spoonful of tomato sauce. Garnish with remaining shaved parmesan, drizzle over a little olive oil and sprinkle with pepper.

braised moroccan-style
baby lamb shanks

This is a perfect dish for a winter dinner party. Because it's so rich and complex, all it really needs is some plain rice or polenta, or some crusty bread and a green salad. Although it's quite time-consuming to make, there's really nothing more therapeutic on a chilly day than roasting spices then pounding them into a paste with fresh aromatics using a pestle and mortar – the fragrance is quite intoxicating! And after its long braising time, the lamb is infused with all the warm, soft flavours of the spices and is meltingly tender.

First, make the paste. Combine saffron with 2 teaspoons of boiling water and set aside. Put fennel seeds, star anise, cardamom pods, cumin seeds, cinnamon and Sichuan peppercorns in a small frying pan and dry-roast over high heat for about 2 minutes, or until fragrant. Pound roasted spices with a pestle and mortar until cardamom is bruised. Discard cardamom husks and keep pounding until all the spices are finely ground. Set aside.

Pound chillies, garlic, ginger, coriander, turmeric and galangal with the pestle and mortar until you have a coarse paste. Add salt and white peppercorns, and pound until peppercorns are lightly crushed. Add shallots, saffron water, paprika, reserved ground spices and oil, and mix well to combine.

Put paste in a medium-sized frying pan and cook over high heat for about 5 minutes, or until fragrant. Reduce heat and simmer gently, stirring occasionally, for 15 minutes. Add palm sugar and fish sauce. Increase heat and simmer, stirring occasionally, for a further 2 minutes, or until mixture is slightly caramelised. Remove from stove and set aside. >

Serve as a main meal for 4

PASTE

small pinch saffron threads

3 teaspoons fennel seeds

2 whole star anise

10 cardamom pods

½ teaspoon cumin seeds

½ cinnamon quill

½ teaspoon Sichuan peppercorns

2 large red chillies, deseeded and roughly chopped

8 garlic cloves, crushed

7 cm (3 in) knob ginger, sliced

¾ cup finely sliced coriander stems and roots

30 g (1 oz) turmeric, finely sliced

75 g (2½ oz) galangal, roughly chopped

2 teaspoons sea salt

1 teaspoon white peppercorns

⅓ cup finely sliced red shallots

¼ teaspoon sweet paprika

1 cup extra virgin olive oil

¼ cup firmly packed palm sugar

¼ cup fish sauce

LAMB SHANKS

8 baby lamb shanks – about 2 kg (4 lb)
in total

pinch sea salt and cracked white pepper

3 medium-sized vine-ripened tomatoes,
roughly chopped

6 kipfler potatoes, peeled and cut
into wedges

2 medium-sized carrots, peeled and
cut into wedges

5 salad onions, trimmed and cut into quarters

4 fresh dates, halved

4 fresh apricots, halved

6 bay leaves

3 cups chicken stock (page 187)

juice of 2 limes

1 tablespoon fish sauce

Meanwhile, preheat oven to 180°C (350°F). Season lamb shanks with salt and pepper and seal in a hot, oiled roasting tin on the stove top until lightly browned on all sides. Drain off any excess oil and drizzle prepared paste over lamb, combining over high heat to coat well and seal in flavours. Add tomatoes, potatoes, carrots, onions, dates, apricots and bay leaves, and stir to combine. Remove tin from stove, pour over stock and cover with foil. Bake for 45 minutes, then remove foil and bake for a further 1 hour, or until lamb is very tender and well browned.

Remove lamb from oven and drizzle with lime juice and fish sauce before serving.

roast duck served with fresh figs, shiitake mushrooms and lime

I just can't go past poaching for its gentleness, and the roasting gives the duck a delightful crispiness, in contrast to the sweetness of figs, the velvety texture of fresh shiitake mushrooms and the zing of fresh lime juice.

Place all stock ingredients in a 10-litre (10-quart) stockpot and bring to the boil. Rinse duck under cold water. Trim away excess fat from inside and outside the cavity, but keep neck, parson's nose and winglets intact. Lower duck, breast-side down, into simmering stock, ensuring it is fully submerged. Reduce heat and poach very gently for exactly 25 minutes, skimming stock regularly with a ladle. Remove from stove and allow duck to steep in stock for 2 hours at room temperature to complete the cooking process. Using tongs, gently remove duck from stock and place breast-side up on a tray to drain and cool. Transfer to a chopping board and, with a cleaver or sharp knife, remove winglets and cut duck in half lengthways. Rub skin with a little sea salt and pepper. Preheat oven to 240°C (500°F). Heat half the oil in a heavy-based frying pan and sear duck halves all over until golden brown. Transfer duck to a roasting tin, drizzle the hot oil over its skin and roast for 8 minutes. Remove from oven, cover with foil and leave to rest in a warm place for 10 minutes.

Meanwhile, remove stems from figs and cut crossways into 1.5 cm (¾ in) thick slices. Heat oil in a frying pan, add garlic and 1 teaspoon of salt and cook, stirring, for 1 minute. Add butter and mushrooms and sauté over high heat for about 2 minutes, or until mushrooms begin to soften. Add sugar and cook, stirring, for a further minute, or until sugar is dissolved and begins to caramelise. Deglaze pan with ½ cup stock, then add figs, vinegar and remaining teaspoon of salt and gently stir to combine and heat through. Remove from stove, add lime juice and pepper, and set aside.

Finally, lay one half of duck on a chopping board. Cut off the wing, then the leg. Remove thigh and breast and cut into slices. Repeat with other half of duck. Arrange duck on a platter and top with the caramelised figs and shiitake mushrooms. Drizzle with remaining olive oil.

Serve as a main meal for 4

1 × 1.75 kg (3½ lb) fresh duck

2 tablespoons extra virgin olive oil

STOCK

6 litres (6 quarts) water

2 cups white wine

3 salad onions, trimmed and sliced

1 small leek, sliced

10 cm (4 in) knob ginger, sliced

12 garlic cloves, crushed

½ bunch flat-leaf parsley, cut in half crossways

¼ cup sea salt

1 tablespoon white sugar

1 tablespoon white peppercorns

8 bay leaves

CARAMELISED FIGS AND SHIITAKE MUSHROOMS

4 medium-sized fresh figs

¼ cup extra virgin olive oil

2 garlic cloves, finely diced

2 teaspoons sea salt

2 tablespoons butter

75 g (2½ oz) fresh shiitake mushrooms, stems discarded and caps sliced

3 teaspoons raw sugar

1 tablespoon red wine vinegar

juice of ½ lime

pinch cracked white pepper

Art and Essence

I love having flowers in the house: their fragrance floods the room, and they lend a kind of freshness and aliveness to everything. When I buy fresh flowers, I often think about the similarities between the worlds of food and flowers – about how we take these living things and, by understanding their essence, turn them into such beautiful creations.

Tracey Deep, who has an amazing florist shop in Paddington, Sydney, is one of the most amazing women I've ever met. She's extremely generous, very talented and she has her heart and soul in the right place. Her arrangements are original and incredibly artistic: she uses palm fronds, soft-green elephant's ear leaves, gnarled bits of wood, weird and wonderful seedpods and gourds of every description, and these delicious, deep-red, velvet-like flowers called cockscombs. She has this beautiful old-fashioned shopfront, and then you walk down these wonderful wooden stairs into a cave-like sandstone area that's cool and moist – just perfect for keeping flowers and arrangements fresh. She works from there each day. And her Lebanese mother, Jeanette, sits alongside her, weaving and wrapping, and basically supporting her. Jeanette does everything so proudly and so willingly and so obligingly, as mothers do.

I feel a special bond with Tracey, even though we haven't known each other long. Maybe it's because we both come from backgrounds where family and food play important roles in our lives. Her mother sitting there reminds me of my grandmother, who always seemed to be sitting in the kitchen when I was growing up, helping my mum prepare meals. Tracey always promises me that she and her mum will cook me dinner one night, which I'm really looking forward to, because I just love Lebanese food!

totally lavish sashimi of kingfish and ocean trout

This recipe came into being because I have an obsession with seafood, because I am addicted to hiramasa (kingfish), and because I love pickled and salty flavours. It is a total celebration of the impeccably fresh seafood available in Australia, and I couldn't resist calling it 'totally lavish' because eating this is like devouring sheets of silk!

Other suitable fish are yellowfin tuna and salmon.

First, make the pickles. Using a mandoline or a very sharp knife, finely slice carrots lengthways into ribbons. Cut onion in half lengthways and finely slice in the same way. Place carrot and onion in a bowl, sprinkle with sugar and salt, and mix well. Cover with plastic wrap and leave to stand for 15 minutes. Add vinegar and fish sauce and stand for a further 15 minutes, or until the vegetables are slightly softened and pickled.

To make the dressing, combine all ingredients except oil in a heatproof bowl. Heat peanut oil in a small pan until moderately hot, then carefully pour over ingredients in bowl to scald them and release their flavours. Stir to combine.

To serve, slice fish into 5 mm (¼ in) slices using a very sharp knife and arrange on a platter with the cucumber. Top with reserved carrot and onion pickles and drizzle with the soy, ginger and chilli dressing before sprinkling with Sichuan pepper and salt.

Serve as a starter for 6

300 g (10 oz) sashimi-grade kingfish fillet

300 g (10 oz) sashimi-grade ocean trout fillet

1 small cucumber, finely sliced lengthways

pinch Sichuan pepper and salt (page 194)

CARROT AND ONION PICKLES

2 small carrots

1 small white onion

1 tablespoon white sugar

2 teaspoons sea salt

½ cup rice wine vinegar

2 teaspoons fish sauce

SOY, GINGER AND CHILLI DRESSING

1 tablespoon ginger julienne

½ cup spring onion (scallion) julienne

1 large red chilli, cut into julienne

2 tablespoons dark soy sauce

1 tablespoon light soy sauce

½ teaspoon sesame oil

1 teaspoon raw sugar

1½ tablespoons chicken stock (page 187)

2 tablespoons peanut oil

salad of foie gras, lobster and soft-boiled duck eggs

Definitely a dish to be reserved for truly special occasions, this decadent dish uses three of my most favourite ingredients – earthy, rich, silky, refined foie gras (try to find Georges Duboeuf brand); sweet, succulent lobster flesh; and rich, runny duck eggs – matched perfectly with crisp beans, delicate French vinegars and best-quality extra virgin olive oil.

If you prefer, you can substitute freshly cooked prawns or crabmeat for the lobster.

Place lobster in the freezer for 1 hour, where it will 'go to sleep', then lower into a large stockpot of boiling salted water and cook for 5 minutes. Using tongs, carefully remove lobster from pot, drain and allow to cool at room temperature. When lobster is cool, remove flesh and slice thickly on the diagonal. Reserve for later use.

Meanwhile, bring a pan of water to the boil, add eggs and boil for 7 minutes. Drain, refresh in cold water, peel and set aside.

Add green beans and butter beans to a pan of boiling salted water and cook until 'al dente'. Drain, refresh in cold water and drain again. Combine beans in a bowl with olive oil, vinegars and salt.

To serve, cut the foie gras into slices and gently tear the eggs in half. Place the mâche on a plate and top with beans, reserving the dressing. Arrange eggs and lobster on the plate, top with foie gras and drizzle with reserved dressing.

Serve as a starter for 4

1 × 700 g (1 lb 6 oz) live lobster

4 free-range duck eggs

60 g (2 oz) baby green beans, trimmed

60 g (2 oz) baby butter beans, trimmed

2 tablespoons extra virgin olive oil

2 teaspoons red wine vinegar

2 teaspoons chardonnay vinegar

1 teaspoon sea salt

75 g (2½ oz) foie gras

handful of mâche (lamb's lettuce) leaves, washed

carpaccio of wagyu beef with rocket, capers and raisins

Serve as a starter for 4

If there's one recipe in this book where you might want to splash out on some Wagyu beef, or at least the very best quality beef fillet, this is it. Because the meat is served raw in this traditional Italian carpaccio, the flavour is paramount – and because it's served in the finest slices, you don't need to buy very much.

⅔ cup finely sliced salad onions

1½ teaspoons white sugar

1 teaspoon sea salt

1½ tablespoons lemon juice

¼ cup raisins, roughly chopped

½ cup extra virgin olive oil

200 g (6½ oz) Wagyu beef fillet, cut into 4 slices

2 small fresh figs

1 tablespoon salted capers, rinsed and drained

30 g (1 oz) Reggiano parmesan, shaved

1–2 handfuls baby rocket (arugula) leaves

Combine onions in a bowl with sugar and salt, mix well and leave to stand for 30 minutes. Add lemon juice and leave for a further 30 minutes, or until the onions are softened and slightly pickled. Stir in raisins and olive oil.

Meanwhile, place a slice of beef on a flat surface between two sheets of plastic wrap. Using a rolling pin, very gently tap and roll the beef until it is an even 2 mm (⅛ in) thickness all over. Peel back one side of the plastic wrap and carefully turn beef out onto a large platter. Repeat with remaining slices of beef.

Remove stems from figs and cut crossways into 5 mm (¼ in) slices. Spoon onion mixture over beef and top with figs. Garnish with capers, parmesan and rocket.

stuffed squid with lime and chilli

The stuffing in this exquisitely tender squid combines Asian and Italian flavours, and the Thai-style dressing is the perfect finishing touch.

Clean squid by gently pulling head and tentacles away from the body. Pull out clear backbone (quill) from inside body and discard entrails. Cut tentacles from head just below the eyes; discard head. Remove side wings and fine membrane from body. Use tentacles and wings for another recipe. Rinse the body well under running water, inside and out, then dry thoroughly with kitchen paper.

To make the stuffing, peel and devein prawns, dice prawn meat and set aside. Pound garlic, ginger and salt with a pestle and mortar until roughly crushed. Heat oil in a heavy-based frying pan, add crushed garlic and ginger and cook over high heat, stirring often, for about 5 minutes, or until soft and aromatic. Reduce heat, add sugar and cook, stirring occasionally, for a further 5 minutes, or until sugar has dissolved and mixture has begun to caramelise. Remove from stove, transfer to a bowl and allow to cool. Stir in reserved prawn meat and all remaining stuffing ingredients.

Preheat oven to 200°C (400°F). Using a small spoon or your fingers, fill squid bodies evenly with stuffing, packing loosely to allow for expansion during cooking. Secure open ends with small bamboo skewers or toothpicks. Arrange squid in a single layer in a roasting tin, then pour over wine and olive oil. Sprinkle with a little salt and pepper, cover dish tightly with foil and bake for 8 minutes. Remove foil and bake for a further 8 minutes, or until squid is lightly browned and just cooked through (test by piercing with the tip of a small knife – it should be opaque all the way through).

Meanwhile, make the dressing. Pound garlic, coriander, ginger, chilli and salt with a pestle and mortar until well crushed but not reduced to a paste. Mix in remaining ingredients.

To serve, remove toothpicks or skewers from squid and cut into slices. Arrange on a platter, drizzle with dressing and garnish with spring onions.

Serve as part of a banquet for 6

12 small whole squid – 1.5 kg (3 lb) in total

⅓ cup white wine

¼ cup extra virgin olive oil

sea salt and cracked white pepper

¼ cup spring onion (scallion) julienne

STUFFING

350 g (11 oz) king prawns (jumbo shrimp)

7 garlic cloves

3 tablespoons roughly chopped ginger

1 teaspoon sea salt

2 tablespoons extra virgin olive oil

2 teaspoons raw sugar

250 g (8 oz) blue eye fillet, diced

⅓ cup diced red shallots

⅓ cup sliced coriander stems and roots

1½ tablespoons diced preserved lemon rind

2 tablespoons diced mustard fruits

1 teaspoon finely grated lime zest

1 tablespoon light soy sauce

¼ cup extra virgin olive oil

DRESSING

3 garlic cloves

1½ tablespoons sliced coriander stems and roots

2 tablespoons chopped ginger

1 large red chilli, deseeded and chopped

1 teaspoon sea salt

1 tablespoon palm sugar

½ cup lime juice

2 tablespoons fish sauce

japanese eggplants with garlic, olive oil and tomatoes

Regular eggplants can be used instead of Japanese eggplants – I just happen to love the shape of Japanese eggplants. With some crusty bread, this makes a great snack or light lunch; it's also delicious as a side dish with a roast chicken or some grilled or roasted fish.

Preheat oven to 180°C (350°F). Halve eggplants lengthways, leaving stems intact. Place eggplants in a single layer, cut-side up, in a lightly oiled roasting tin. Drizzle with olive oil, sprinkle with garlic, thyme sprigs and salt, and cover tin with foil. Bake for 45 minutes, or until eggplants are tender.

Remove from oven and increase temperature to 200°C (400°F). Drizzle eggplants with half the extra oil and bake, uncovered, for a further 15 minutes, or until lightly browned.

Arrange eggplants on a platter and top with tomatoes. Drizzle with remaining oil and lemon juice, sprinkle with salt and pepper, and serve.

Serve as a side dish for 6

550 g (1 lb 2 oz) Japanese eggplants (aubergines)

⅓ cup extra virgin olive oil

7 garlic cloves, finely diced

¼ bunch thyme

1 teaspoon sea salt

2 tablespoons extra virgin olive oil, extra

2 medium-sized vine-ripened tomatoes, finely sliced

juice of 1 lemon

pinch sea salt

pinch cracked white pepper

marinated lamb racks with blood plum and balsamic onion relish

Serve as a main meal for 4

1 tablespoon white peppercorns

½ cup extra virgin olive oil

¼ cup roughly chopped rosemary leaves

1 tablespoon sea salt

2 × 450 g (14 oz) lamb racks, each with 8 bones

RELISH

⅓ cup extra virgin olive oil

4 medium-sized red onions, finely sliced

6 garlic cloves, finely diced

1 tablespoon sea salt

⅓ cup white sugar

⅔ cup balsamic vinegar

6 ripe blood plums, halved

1 tablespoon lemon juice

The sweet, tangy relish in this recipe really brings out the flavours of the lamb. If you have some relish left over, it will keep well for up to a month in the fridge, and is delicious with any grilled meat or in sandwiches.

Using a pestle and mortar, pound peppercorns until lightly crushed. Combine peppercorns with oil, rosemary and salt in a large, shallow dish. Trim fat from exposed bones of the lamb racks. Add lamb to the marinade, using your hands to rub the marinade well into the meat. Cover and refrigerate for 2 hours.

Meanwhile, make the relish. Heat oil in a medium-sized, heavy-based pan. Add onions, garlic and salt, cook, stirring occasionally, over medium heat for about 20 minutes, or until onions are soft. Lower heat, add sugar and cook, stirring often, for a further 10 minutes. Pour in vinegar and simmer, uncovered, stirring occasionally, for about 30 minutes, or until onions are very soft and sweet. Add plums, simmer for a further 15 minutes, or until plums are just tender. Remove pan from the stove, stir in lemon juice and set aside.

Preheat oven to 200°C (400°F). Place a lightly oiled frying pan over high heat and seal lamb racks until lightly browned all over. Transfer to a roasting tin and pour hot pan juices over the lamb, along with any remaining marinade. Roast, uncovered, for about 10 minutes, or until cooked as desired. Remove from oven, cover with foil and leave to rest in a warm place for 10 minutes. Reserve pan juices.

Using a sharp knife, cut lamb racks into cutlets and arrange on plates. Drizzle the lamb with reserved pan juices, and serve with a bowl of relish on the side.

bruny island mussels cooked in white wine, french butter, orange and saffron

I like to use Bruny Island mussels for this dish. They come from the crystal-clear waters that surround Bruny Island, just south of Hobart, in Tasmania, and they have the purest flavour. Of course, if you can't get these, just buy the freshest black-lipped mussels you can find – look for heavy, shiny mussels with a very clean smell. When cooking mussels, be very, very careful not to overcook them; you want them to be plump and juicy. They really don't take long at all to cook, so make sure you have everything prepared before you start cooking. Because this recipe is a homage to traditional French cuisine, I like to use French butter (when in France, do as the French do!), but any good-quality butter is fine. Served with crusty bread to mop up the juices, and perhaps a green salad on the side, this makes a lovely light meal.

Scrub, debeard, rinse and drain the mussels, then set aside. Combine saffron with 2 teaspoons of boiling water in a small bowl and set aside.

Melt half the butter in a large, heavy-based, shallow pan. Add carrots, fennel, onions, ginger and salt. Gently sauté, covered, over low heat for about 15 minutes, or until vegetables have softened but not coloured. Stir often to prevent the vegetables catching on the bottom of the pan.

Add remaining butter, together with wine, orange juice, extra salt and the saffron water. Bring to the boil, then stir in reserved mussels and orange zest. Reduce heat and simmer gently, covered, for 3 minutes. Scatter over the tomato and herbs and continue cooking, covered, for a further minute, or until the mussels have just opened (discard any that won't open). Remove from heat immediately, and serve.

Serve as a main meal for 4–6

1.5 kg (3 lb) live mussels

small pinch saffron threads

100 g (3½ oz) unsalted French butter

2 small carrots, peeled and finely sliced on the diagonal

2 baby fennel bulbs, trimmed and finely sliced

½ cup finely sliced salad onions

2 tablespoons finely julienned ginger

1 teaspoon sea salt

¾ cup white wine

½ cup freshly squeezed orange juice

1 tablespoon sea salt, extra

2 teaspoons finely grated orange zest

1 small ox-heart (beef) tomato, finely sliced

¼ cup roughly chopped mint

¼ cup roughly chopped flat-leaf parsley

roast wagyu beef fillet served with sweet and sour red radish salad

Serve as a starter for 4

The caramel texture and sweet, rich flavours of this marinade are perfectly complemented by the sweet and sour, light and vibrant red radish salad. Because the beef is served quite rare in this recipe, you should use the best-quality beef fillet you can find, to ensure tenderness.

2 × 200 g (6½ oz) pieces Wagyu beef fillet

2 tablespoons vegetable oil

dash of extra virgin olive oil

MARINADE

2 tablespoons kecap manis

½ cup shao hsing wine

1 tablespoon white sugar

½ tablespoon sesame oil

2 tablespoons light soy sauce

2 tablespoons Chinese black vinegar

SWEET AND SOUR RADISH SALAD

3 garlic cloves, peeled

1 tablespoon extra virgin olive oil

4 red radishes, finely sliced

1 small red onion, finely sliced

¼ cup red wine vinegar

2 teaspoons white sugar

1 tablespoon sea salt

Combine beef with marinade ingredients in a large bowl, cover and refrigerate for 3 hours.

Next, make the salad. Crush garlic with a mortar and pestle, add olive oil and grind into a paste. Transfer paste to a bowl and combine with all remaining salad ingredients. Cover and refrigerate for 1 hour.

Preheat oven to 220°C (450°F). Remove beef from marinade and drain; discard marinade. Heat vegetable oil in a heavy-based frying pan. Cook beef for about 2 minutes, or until well browned on one side. Turn over and briefly seal the other side, then remove immediately.

Transfer beef to a roasting tin and cook for about 4 minutes, or until rare. Remove from oven, cover with foil and leave to rest in a warm place for 10 minutes.

To serve, cut beef into 1 cm (½ in) thick slices and arrange on a platter. Top with sweet and sour radish salad and drizzle with a little olive oil.

poached chicken and king prawn salad with mustard fruits, celery and lemon

I created this recipe around my love for Italian mustard fruits, which I first stumbled across in a wonderful book called *Savouring Italy*, by Robert Freson. Made of various whole fruits preserved in a thick, mustard-flavoured syrup, in this dish their robust nature is balanced by the silky texture of poached chicken, the delicate sweetness of prawns and the sharpness of lemon juice.

Pour tea over raisins and leave to stand for 20 minutes, or until soft. Drain, reserving fruit and discarding tea.

Combine onions in a bowl with salt and sugar, mix well and leave to stand for 30 minutes. Add lemon juice and leave to stand for a further 30 minutes, or until onions are softened and slightly pickled.

Add prawns to a large pan of boiling salted water and boil for 2–3 minutes. Drain, refresh in iced water and drain immediately. Peel and devein prawns, then cut in half on the diagonal.

Add celery to a pan of boiling salted water and blanch for 30 seconds. Drain, refresh under cold water and drain again.

Using your hands, tear meat from chicken in large pieces and place in a bowl with raisins, onions, prawns, celery, mustard fruits, lemon zest, extra salt, oil, vinegar and parsley. Arrange salad on a platter, drizzle with extra olive oil and sprinkle with pepper.

Serve as a starter for 4–6

½ cup hot black tea

⅓ cup raisins

1 cup finely sliced salad onions

1 teaspoon sea salt

1 teaspoon white sugar

⅓ cup lemon juice

500 g (1 lb) uncooked king prawns (jumbo shrimp)

2 small sticks of celery, sliced on the diagonal

1 × 1.5 kg (3 lb) 'kylie's poached chicken' (page 190)

¼ cup finely sliced mustard fruits

2 teaspoons finely grated lemon zest

2 teaspoons sea salt, extra

1 tablespoon extra virgin olive oil

2 teaspoons chardonnay vinegar

½ cup flat-leaf parsley leaves

dash of extra virgin olive oil, extra

pinch cracked white pepper

freshly poached lobster served with roast baby beetroot, braised leeks and fennel

I love the textures and colours in this dish – I especially like the way such a sophisticated ingredient as lobster teams perfectly with humble, peasant-style vegetables. This rich and decadent dish is best served in small portions as a starter.

Place lobster in freezer for 1 hour, where it will 'go to sleep', then lower into a large stockpot of boiling salted water and cook for 5 minutes. Using tongs, carefully remove lobster from pot, drain and allow to cool at room temperature.

Preheat oven to 180°C (350°F). Place beetroot in a roasting tin, drizzle with half the olive oil and sprinkle with half the salt and pepper. Cover tin with foil and bake for about 1½–2 hours, or until tender. Trim roots and tips from leeks and cut crossways into 10 cm (4 in) lengths. Place leeks in a separate roasting tin, drizzle with remaining oil, chardonnay vinegar and balsamic vinegar, and sprinkle with remaining salt and pepper. Cover tin with foil and bake for about 35 minutes, or until tender.

While the beetroot and leeks are roasting, prepare the mayonnaise and the fennel salad. For the mayonnaise, place egg yolks, mustard, salt and sugar in a bowl and lightly whisk to combine. Gradually add oil in a thin stream, whisking continuously until you have a thick mayonnaise. Stir in lemon juice, vinegar and a little pepper. For the fennel salad, combine all the ingredients in a bowl and leave to stand for 10 minutes.

Remove beetroot and leeks from oven. When beetroot is cool enough to handle, peel and cut into 1 cm (½ in) thick slices. Leave leeks in roasting tin with their juices.

To serve, remove cooked meat from lobster and slice thickly on the diagonal. Arrange lobster, beetroot and the fennel salad on a serving platter and top with the leeks, reserving their juices. Place a dollop of mayonnaise on the leeks and drizzle over reserved juices from roasting tin.

Serve as a starter for 4–6

1 × 750 g (1½ lb) live lobster

300 g (10 oz) fresh baby beetroot – about 1 bunch – trimmed

½ cup extra virgin olive oil

1 teaspoon sea salt

pinch cracked white pepper

200 g (6½ oz) baby leeks

1 tablespoon chardonnay vinegar

1 tablespoon balsamic vinegar

MAYONNAISE

2 egg yolks

1 teaspoon Dijon mustard

1 teaspoon sea salt

½ teaspoon white sugar

½ cup extra virgin olive oil

1 tablespoon lemon juice

1 teaspoon chardonnay vinegar

pinch cracked white pepper

FENNEL SALAD

1 baby fennel bulb, trimmed and very finely sliced

1 tablespoon extra virgin olive oil

2 teaspoons lemon juice

1 teaspoon sea salt

Simplicity and Richness

When I create new recipes, I draw inspiration from going to the food markets and seeing the abundance of fresh produce. One of the greatest gifts I took away from my six years working with Neil Perry was an absolute passion for quality and an understanding of the importance of using the best, freshest ingredients. Of course, Chinese people have an absolute obsession with fresh produce – whether it's seafood or meat or vegetables – so I didn't need much persuasion.

Neil also taught me the importance of cultivating good relationships with providores. John Susman, my beloved friend and the most passionate of fishmongers, acts as my eyes and ears at the fish markets. To nurture my relationship with John, I always make sure that he and his family are well fed! There is nothing more delightful than watching his two gorgeous and sweet little sons, Harry and Georgie, devour some crispy prawn wontons. Frankie Theodore and Mark Eather are my other two seafood providores, and it feels like Christmas every day when the Hawkesbury River calamari, whole line-caught bar cod and the juiciest, plumpest Tasmanian oysters all arrive at once. Hand-picked, highest-quality fruit and vegetables from Hughie Wennerbon and Justyn McGrigor invigorate every stir-fry and salad. Anthony and Victor Puharich, our butchers, embody warmth and generosity, and I love them because they understand the Chinese penchant for unusual cuts of meat and 'fatty bits'! Myriam Cordellier produces the most stunning sourdough bread in Australia, and my Uncle Jimmy continues the Jang family tradition of producing the freshest egg noodles and wonton wrappers.

My other source of inspiration is the rich treasure-trove of food writing and recipe books that line my shelves at home. I pore over my cookbooks – especially those by Stephanie Alexander, Elizabeth David, Claudia Roden, Maggie Beer, Joel Robuchon and Alice Waters, and my ever-expanding collection of Italian, Greek and Mediterranean cookbooks. But my greatest inspiration comes simply from the things I most love to cook, and sharing them with people in beautiful surroundings.

les oeufs modestes

This recipe is very humble and satisfying – hence the name, which means 'modest eggs'. Either duck eggs or hen eggs will suffice, as long as they are fresh. To soft-boil duck eggs, bring water to the boil, then add eggs and cook for 7 minutes; remove and refresh in iced water. For hen eggs, reduce the cooking time to 4 minutes.

Wash asparagus and snap off and discard woody ends. Peel lower parts of stems. Add asparagus to boiling salted water and cook until 'al dente' – about 3 minutes. Drain, then plunge asparagus into a large bowl of iced water for 30 seconds; drain well. Slice asparagus on the diagonal.

Carefully peel the eggs, cut in half and arrange on a platter with the asparagus. Garnish with herbs and drizzle with olive oil and lemon juice. Sprinkle with salt and pepper.

Serve as a starter for 4

8 large green asparagus spears

6 soft-boiled free-range eggs

2 teaspoons finely chopped dill

1½ tablespoons finely chopped flat-leaf parsley

¼ cup extra virgin olive oil

2 teaspoons lemon juice

pinch sea salt

pinch cracked white pepper

sashimi of yellowfin tuna and tasmanian scallops

Use only the best and freshest tuna and scallops for this recipe. I have a weakness for yellowfin tuna and the delectable scallops that thrive in the cool waters off Tasmania, but any good-quality tuna and very fresh scallops will do.

Clean the scallops, but leave them attached to their shells.

Using a very sharp knife, cut the tuna into 5 mm (¼ in) slices and arrange on a platter, with the scallops and tomato on the side. Drizzle with the oil and vinegar and garnish with chervil, salt and pepper.

Serve as a starter for 4

8 live Tasmanian sea scallops

375 g (12 oz) sashimi-grade yellowfin tuna

½ small ox-heart (beef) tomato, finely sliced

2 tablespoons extra virgin olive oil

1 tablespoon balsamic vinegar

1 tablespoon picked chervil leaves

½ teaspoon sea salt

pinch cracked white pepper

pan-cooked blue eye served with kipfler potatoes and sage

Serve as a main meal for 4

I first discovered the magical combination of sage and burnt butter when I sampled Franca Manfredi's handmade spinach and ricotta gnocchi drizzled with burnt butter and sage. The rich, nutty flavour is heavenly in this recipe, and the shiitake mushrooms just drink it up. Combined with the vivacious taste of ripe tomatoes and the waxy, earthy flavour of kipfler potatoes, this makes a rich and flavoursome counterpoint to the dense flesh of blue eye. Other suitable fish for this dish include cod, hake and monkfish.

2 medium-sized vine-ripened tomatoes

125 g (4 oz) unsalted butter

5 medium-sized kipfler potatoes, peeled and sliced into 1 cm ($\frac{1}{2}$ in) rounds

75 g ($2\frac{1}{2}$ oz) fresh shiitake mushrooms, stems discarded

1 teaspoon sea salt

8 fresh sage leaves

4 × 100 g ($3\frac{1}{2}$ oz) blue eye fillets

pinch cracked white pepper and sea salt

dash of extra virgin olive oil

Using a small knife, cut a shallow cross in the base of each tomato. Bring a pan of water to the boil and plunge tomatoes in the water for 30 seconds. Using a slotted spoon, remove tomatoes quickly and refresh in a bowl of cold water. Drain, then peel away the skin and cut tomatoes into quarters, discarding seeds and juices.

Melt butter in a medium-sized frying pan, add potatoes and sauté over medium heat for about 10 minutes, or until tender, lightly browned and crisp. Stir in mushrooms and salt, and cook, stirring occasionally, for a further 5 minutes, or until mushrooms are tender. Add sage, cook for a further 1 minute then remove from heat.

Meanwhile, cook the fish in a heated, oiled frying pan until lightly browned on both sides and just cooked through – about 3–4 minutes. Remove from pan, cover with foil and leave to rest in a warm place for 3 minutes.

To serve, place potatoes and mushrooms on a platter and top with the reserved tomato quarters. Arrange fish on top, sprinkle with pepper and salt and drizzle with a little olive oil.

king prawn and scallop omelette with tomato and chilli dressing

This recipe is very simple, quick and delicious – the fresh filling of greens and herbs helps to cut through the richness of the omelette.

For the omelette filling, finely julienne snow peas and blanch in boiling salted water until 'al dente' – about 30 seconds. Drain, refresh in cold water, then thoroughly drain again. In a bowl, combine snow peas with sprouts, chives, cloud ear fungus, herbs and spring onion. Set aside.

To make the dressing, combine vinegar and sugar together in a small pan and stir over low heat until sugar is dissolved (do not allow to boil). Simmer, uncovered and without stirring, for about 10 minutes, or until mixture is reduced by half. Meanwhile, pound chillies and salt into a rough paste with a pestle and mortar. Add tomato and crush slightly to release the juices. Pour in ½ cup of the warm vinegar and sugar syrup, and the fish sauce, mix well and set aside.

Peel and devein prawns, leaving tails intact. Butterfly the prawns by making a shallow cut along the back (this helps them to cook quickly and evenly), then season them with salt and pepper. Clean scallops and cut them away from the shell, keeping the coral intact. Heat a little oil in a frying pan and cook prawns until lightly browned. Add scallops to the same pan and cook on both sides until lightly browned. Transfer prawns and scallops to a warm plate and cover with foil to keep warm while you make the omelette.

Combine eggs and water in a bowl and beat lightly with a fork. Heat 2 tablespoons of oil in a non-stick frying pan about 23 cm (9 in) in diameter over high heat. Pour in egg mixture, tilting pan so mixture coats base evenly. Cook over medium heat for about 2 minutes, loosening edges with a fish slice, until omelette is lightly browned underneath and almost set. Quickly place filling and half the prawns and scallops on one half of the omelette, fold over the other half to enclose the filling and carefully slide onto a serving platter. Garnish with remaining prawns and scallops. Serve immediately, with a bowl of tomato and chilli dressing on the side.

Serve as a starter for 2–4

60 g (2 oz) snow peas (mange-tout), trimmed

1 cup bean sprouts

⅓ bunch garlic chives, trimmed and cut into thirds crossways

⅓ cup fresh black cloud ear fungus

¼ cup mint leaves

¼ cup flat-leaf parsley leaves

¼ cup spring onion (scallion) julienne

4 uncooked king prawns (jumbo shrimp)

pinch sea salt and cracked white pepper

8 sea scallops on the half-shell

vegetable oil for frying

3 free-range duck eggs or 4 free-range hen eggs

2 teaspoons water

TOMATO AND CHILLI DRESSING

1 cup rice wine vinegar

½ cup white sugar

1 large red chilli, deseeded and roughly sliced

2 teaspoons sea salt

1 small ox-heart (beef) tomato, roughly chopped

2 tablespoons fish sauce

pan-cooked snapper fillet with tea-scented sour cherry and tomato salad

Serve as a main meal for 4

In Chinese cuisine, snapper is often steamed with ginger and spring onions to complement its refined, delicate flavour and texture. Cooked Western-style, snapper benefits from minimal cooking and a fresh, light yet interesting accompaniment. The dried cherries are wonderfully chewy, with a slightly salty and sour flavour. Soaking half of them in jasmine tea not only creates a different texture, but also imparts a subtle jasmine scent, and the tomato salad gives the whole dish a refreshing edge.

1 tablespoon jasmine tea leaves

$\frac{1}{4}$ cup dried sour cherries

1 small red onion, finely sliced

1 garlic clove, finely diced

1 teaspoon sea salt

1 teaspoon raw sugar

3 medium-sized vine-ripened tomatoes

2 teaspoons red wine vinegar

1 teaspoon chardonnay vinegar

2 tablespoons extra virgin olive oil

pinch cracked white pepper

4 × 100 g (3½ oz) snapper fillets

dash of extra virgin olive oil, extra

Put tea leaves in a bowl, pour over $\frac{1}{4}$ cup of boiling water, cover and leave to stand for 5 minutes. Strain, discarding tea leaves and returning liquid to the bowl, along with half the cherries. Leave to stand for 20 minutes, then strain and reserve cherries, discarding liquid.

Place onion and garlic in another bowl, sprinkle with salt and sugar and mix well. Cover and leave to stand for 20 minutes.

Meanwhile, using a small knife, cut a shallow cross in the base of each tomato. Bring a pan of water to the boil and plunge tomatoes in the water for 30 seconds. Using a slotted spoon, remove tomatoes quickly and refresh in a bowl of cold water. Drain, then peel away skin and cut tomatoes into quarters, discarding seeds and juices.

Add combined vinegars, oil, pepper, soaked cherries, remaining dried cherries and tomato quarters to the onion mixture.

Finally, cook the fish in a heated, oiled frying pan until lightly browned on both sides and just cooked through – about 3–4 minutes. Remove fish from the pan, cover with foil and leave to rest in a warm place for 3 minutes.

Arrange fish on a platter, top with tomato mixture and drizzle with a little olive oil.

french-style braised octopus

Many years ago, when Neil Perry and his business partner Trish Richards owned a French restaurant in Sydney, I begged them to let me work there, because I felt my lack of formal training and was desperate to learn some classical French cuisine. It was there that I learnt to cook this delicious Provençale braised octopus. It's beautiful warm or at room temperature, and it makes a lovely lunch with some crusty bread and a great bottle of red. I really love the smoky bacon bones in this recipe – get your butcher to saw them into slices for you.

To clean octopus, cut tentacles away from head below the beak. Cut away and discard the beak, then turn the body inside out. Remove ink sac and internal organs. Strip skin away from head and tentacles under running water. Rinse and drain well, then cut octopus in half.

Pound garlic, chopped ginger and salt with a pestle and mortar until crushed. Stir in vinegar and oil. Place octopus in a bowl and pour over garlic mixture and honey. Using your hands, mix thoroughly. Cover and refrigerate for 1 hour.

Meanwhile, peel carrots, cut into quarters lengthways and slice. Cut celery sticks in half lengthways and slice. Heat extra oil in a large, heavy-based pan, add sliced ginger, carrots, celery, onions, fennel, bacon bones and extra salt. Cook over high heat, stirring occasionally, for 5 minutes. Reduce heat and cook for a further 10 minutes, or until vegetables are lightly browned. Add thyme and sugar, increase heat again and cook, stirring occasionally, for a further 2 minutes.

Drain octopus from marinade; reserve marinade. Add octopus to pan and stir over high heat to sear octopus and seal in juices. Pour in reserved marinade, along with wine, and bring to the boil. Reduce heat and simmer gently, covered, for about 45 minutes, or until octopus is tender.

Serve as a main meal for 6

1.5 kg (3 lb) baby octopus

10 garlic cloves

5 cm (2 in) knob ginger, roughly chopped

1 teaspoon sea salt

½ cup sherry vinegar

⅓ cup extra virgin olive oil

¼ cup honey

3 medium-sized carrots

3 sticks of celery

1 cup extra virgin olive oil, extra

6 cm (2½ in) knob ginger, sliced

8 small salad onions, trimmed and cut into quarters

1 baby fennel bulb, finely sliced lengthways

150 g (5 oz) smoked bacon bones, sliced

1 tablespoon sea salt, extra

½ bunch thyme

¼ cup raw sugar

⅓ cup red wine

pan-cooked blue eye served with hot saffron and ginger tomato sauce

Serve as a main meal for 4

I love the subtle yet distinctive flavour of saffron, and I also love the way it intensifies the colour of the sauces to which it is added. My inspiration for this sauce comes from the Middle East. Even though it is simple to prepare, it is rather complex and interesting in flavour – with heat from the chilli, sourness from the lemon and a liquorice taste from the fennel.

Monkfish or cod can also be used in this recipe.

pinch saffron threads

750 g (1½ lb) ox-heart (beef) tomatoes, roughly chopped

1½ tablespoons ginger julienne

2 teaspoons finely sliced preserved lemon rind

1½ teaspoons sea salt

1 red bird's eye chilli, sliced

1 baby fennel bulb, trimmed and very finely sliced

1 tablespoon extra virgin olive oil

1 teaspoon balsamic vinegar

1 teaspoon sea salt, extra

4 × 100 g (3½ oz) blue eye fillets

dash of extra virgin olive oil, extra

pinch cracked white pepper

Combine saffron with 2 teaspoons of boiling water in a small bowl and set aside. Lightly crush tomatoes with a pestle and mortar until they release their juices. Put crushed tomatoes in a heavy-based frying pan, along with ginger, preserved lemon rind, salt, saffron water and chilli. Simmer over low heat for about 40 minutes, or until sauce is slightly reduced and thickened. Season with a little pepper.

Meanwhile, combine fennel with olive oil, vinegar and extra salt, and set aside.

Cook fish in a heated, oiled frying pan until lightly browned on both sides and just cooked through – about 3–4 minutes. Remove fish from pan, cover with foil and leave to rest in a warm place for 3 minutes.

To serve, spoon the sauce onto a platter, arrange fish on the sauce and top with reserved fennel salad. Drizzle dish with a little olive oil and sprinkle with pepper.

pork cutlets served with braised red cabbage and green apples

This combination of pork and cabbage is a classic one. I especially like the depth of flavour in the braised cabbage: the bacon imparts smokiness and the orange zest infuses the cabbage with a delicious bitterness. I love using organic pork cutlets because of their fresh, clean flavour and juiciness – the addition of green apples reminds me of my nanna, for some reason, and their sweetness balances out the lovely sourness of the vinegar.

Preheat oven to 200°C (400°F).

Heat oil in a heavy-based frying pan. Add bacon, shallots, garlic and half the salt, and sauté over high heat for about 5 minutes, or until bacon is lightly browned and crisp. Add cabbage and capsicum and sauté for a further 3 minutes. Add sugar and cook, stirring, for about 2 minutes, or until mixture starts to caramelise. Add wine, vinegar, apples, bay leaves, orange zest and remaining salt. Cook gently, covered, for about 20 minutes, stirring occasionally, until cabbage is softened.

Meanwhile, drizzle pork cutlets with the extra olive oil and seal on both sides, in a hot frying pan, until golden brown. Transfer pork to a roasting tin and bake for about 8 minutes, or until just cooked through. Remove from oven and leave to rest in a warm place for 10 minutes. Remove pork from roasting tin and slice, reserving pan juices.

To serve, arrange pork on a platter with the braised cabbage. Drizzle with reserved pan juices and sprinkle with pepper.

Serve as a main meal for 4

¼ cup extra virgin olive oil

125 g (4 oz) bacon with rind, cut into 1 cm (½ in) dice

8 golden shallots, finely sliced

4 garlic cloves, roughly chopped

1 tablespoon sea salt

½ red cabbage, finely sliced

1 red capsicum (bell pepper), cut into julienne

5 teaspoons raw sugar

½ cup red wine

2 tablespoons red wine vinegar

2 tablespoons sherry vinegar

4 small green apples, peeled, cored and grated

3 bay leaves

2 teaspoons finely grated orange zest

4 × 200 g (6½ oz) organic pork cutlets

2 tablespoons extra virgin olive oil, extra

pinch cracked white pepper

braised chicken with vibrant flavours

Serve as a main meal for 4–6

This is a rustic dish that can be cooked in advance and then just reheated and served in a big earthenware pot. The vibrant flavours come from global influences – it's got a little bit of French in it, a little bit of Thai and a little bit of Moroccan. The colours are no less vibrant, with bright red tomatoes and the golden hue of saffron.

Serve with crusty sourdough bread.

small pinch saffron threads

⅓ cup plain (all-purpose) flour

½ teaspoon sea salt

pinch cracked white pepper

1.5 kg (3 lb) organic chicken thighs on the bone, with skin

1 cup olive oil

6 cm (2½ in) knob ginger, sliced

20 g (¾ oz) turmeric, finely diced

10 garlic cloves, crushed

1 tablespoon sea salt, extra

3 small carrots, peeled and cut into chunks

6 small red shallots, peeled

5 small roma (plum) tomatoes

6 bay leaves

5 tablespoons palm sugar

¼ cup fish sauce

1 tablespoon finely sliced preserved lemon rind

6 fresh dates, halved and pitted

5 large red chillies, bruised

1 teaspoon ground cumin

1 lime, cut into quarters

½ cup red wine

½ cup sherry vinegar

juice of 1 lime

Combine saffron with 2 teaspoons of boiling water in a small bowl and set aside.

Combine flour with salt and pepper, then toss chicken in seasoned flour to thoroughly coat, shaking away excess. Heat olive oil in large frying pan and shallow-fry chicken, in batches, until lightly browned on all sides. Remove from pan and drain on kitchen paper. Set aside.

Add ginger, turmeric, garlic and extra salt to remaining oil in the same pan and cook over medium heat, stirring, for about 1 minute, or until fragrant. Add carrots, shallots, whole tomatoes and bay leaves, stirring well to coat vegetables in the oil mixture. Add palm sugar and cook, stirring, for a further minute, or until mixture begins to caramelise. Stir in fish sauce and bring to the boil. Add preserved lemon rind, dates, chillies, cumin, lime quarters and reserved saffron water. Stir to combine, then pour in wine and vinegar and simmer over high heat for 2 minutes.

Finally, return chicken to the pan and reduce heat. Simmer gently, covered, for about 40 minutes, or until chicken is just cooked through and vegetables are tender. Drizzle chicken with lime juice before serving.

blue eye and king prawns with lemon and honey onions

The combination of salty, sweet and sour flavours is evident in so many cuisines – Asian, Middle Eastern, European – and it's a trio of tastes that I adore. In this recipe, the lemon and honey onions work as a beautiful relish for the sweet, delicate flavours of the prawns and fish.

In cooler climes, haddock or cod can be substituted for the blue eye.

Peel and devein the prawns, but leave the tail intact – you should have about 350 g (11 oz). Reserve heads and shells for stock. Butterfly the prawns by making a shallow cut along the back – this helps them to cook quickly and evenly.

For the stock, pound garlic, ginger and salt with a pestle and mortar until you have a fine paste. Heat oil in a small, heavy-based pan, add garlic paste, celery, carrot and lemongrass, and sauté for 2 minutes, or until aromatic. Stir in tomatoes and parsley, then add reserved prawn heads and shells and sauté for 1 minute. Pour in wine and simmer for 2 minutes, or until alcohol has evaporated. Add 1 cup of water and simmer, uncovered, for 20 minutes. Have ready a fine strainer over a large bowl. Ladle stock into strainer, gently pressing the ingredients to extract as much liquid as possible. Set aside.

For the onions, heat oil in a frying pan and add onions and salt. Sauté for about 2 minutes, or until onions are lightly browned. Add honey, reduce heat and simmer gently over low heat for 2 minutes. Add lemon juice and simmer, uncovered, for about 10 minutes, or until slightly thickened and caramelised.

Season prawns with a little salt and pepper, and cook in a heated, oiled frying pan until lightly browned and just tender. Remove prawns from pan and cover with foil to keep warm while you poach the fish.

Return stock to a small pan and bring to the boil; add fish pieces and reduce heat. Poach very gently, uncovered, for about 3 minutes, or until just tender. Place sliced tomato in the centre of a large, shallow bowl and arrange prawns and fish on top. Spoon over the stock and top with the onions. Garnish with parsley and serve immediately.

Serve as part of a banquet for 4

750 g (1½ lb) uncooked king prawns (jumbo shrimp)

pinch sea salt and cracked pepper

400 g (13 oz) blue eye fillet, cut into large pieces

1 medium-sized ox-heart (beef) tomato, roughly sliced

¼ cup chopped flat-leaf parsley

STOCK

3 garlic cloves

8 slices ginger

1 tablespoon sea salt

½ cup olive oil

1 stick of celery, sliced

1 small carrot, peeled and finely diced

1½ tablespoons sliced lemongrass

2 medium-sized vine-ripened tomatoes, sliced

¼ bunch flat-leaf parsley, cut in half crossways

½ cup white wine

LEMON AND HONEY ONIONS

1½ tablespoons extra virgin olive oil

10 small salad onions, trimmed

1 small red onion, sliced

½ teaspoon sea salt

2 tablespoons honey

1 tablespoon lemon juice

Sharing
and Celebrating

I have had countless dinner parties in my life, and I look forward to so many more. I think cooking for family and friends is a wonderful expression of love and how we feel about people. Not just the cooking, but the whole process: going to the markets and seeking out the best produce; taking time to prepare the food in a respectful and appropriate manner; taking the time to set the table beautifully; lighting the candles and polishing the glasses – the whole ritual. It is an opportunity to embrace the more important things in life, such as sharing and celebrating.

It was my birthday in March, and my mother and my brothers generously offered to cook me dinner. So we had an amazing night at my house, with all these adorable little children running around chuckling and carrying on, screaming and yelping as they cut the cake in all sorts of weird and wonky ways. There was plenty of food. Mum cooked her famous roast chicken and roast vegetables, and my dining-room table groaned under the weight of candles, flowers and big platters of food. My nephew and niece had made me a beautiful birthday cake, iced in rainbow colours and, of course, there were candles to be blown out and sparklers to be lit, which the children got very excited about.

But, for me, the most important thing was that I was surrounded by my family, and the whole night was incredibly joyous. I just sort of sat quietly and noticed everyone and every moment. I thought about all the other birthdays and celebrations to come, and I felt inspired and contented, knowing that the children in our family will grow up living life from the heart and soul.

steamboat

A traditional Chinese steamboat, where diners choose from an array of raw and marinated ingredients to dip into simmering stock, is a brilliant example of the art of interaction, of sharing and socialising. Imagine your friends sitting around a ferociously steaming wok: their eyes will be treated to a vista of the freshest, most colourful food; their noses will be tantalised by the aromas of the most fragrant herbs; and their tastebuds will be rapt with the variety of tastes and textures.

Because the meat is only lightly cooked, it is definitely preferable to use organic meats for a steamboat – the flavour will be so much better. Suitable fish include blue eye, snapper, halibut and sea bass. Salted radish and pickled mustard greens, which you'll need for the dipping sauces, are available at Asian supermarkets, as are salted duck eggs.

Clean squid by gently pulling head and tentacles away from the body. Pull out the clear backbone (quill) from inside the body and discard entrails. Cut tentacles from the head just below the eyes; discard head. Remove side wings and fine membrane from the body. Rinse body, tentacles and wings thoroughly and pat dry with kitchen paper.

Cut the squid down the centre so that it will open out flat. Using a small, sharp knife, score shallow diagonal cuts in a criss-cross pattern on the inside surface. Cut scored squid into 5 x 2.5 cm (2 x 1 in) pieces and place in a bowl.

For the squid marinade, pound chilli and salt into a rough paste with a pestle and mortar. Add palm sugar, pound lightly, then stir in fish sauce, ginger and lime juice. Add marinade to the squid in the bowl.

Place pork, chicken, beef, fish and prawns in separate bowls, then set aside while you prepare the garlic and ginger paste.

Pound garlic, ginger and salt together with a pestle and mortar until you have a rough paste. Divide this paste between the pork, chicken and beef.

Serve with steamed rice as a main meal for 6

700 g (1 lb 6 oz) small whole squid

SQUID MARINADE

2 large red chillies, halved lengthways, deseeded and roughly sliced

1 teaspoon sea salt

1½ tablespoons palm sugar

1 tablespoon fish sauce

2 tablespoons ginger julienne

1 tablespoon lime juice

300 g (10 oz) organic pork fillet, finely sliced on the diagonal

300 g (10 oz) organic chicken fillet, finely sliced on the diagonal

300 g (10 oz) organic beef fillet, finely sliced on the diagonal

400 g (13 oz) white fish fillets, finely sliced on the diagonal

12 uncooked king prawns (jumbo shrimp), peeled and deveined but with tails intact

GARLIC AND GINGER PASTE

10 garlic cloves, crushed

½ cup roughly chopped ginger

1 teaspoon sea salt

PORK MARINADE

2 tablespoons hoisin sauce

1 tablespoon shao hsing wine

1 teaspoon Chinese black vinegar

dash of sesame oil

Add the five lots of marinade ingredients for the pork, chicken, beef, fish and prawns to their respective bowls. Thoroughly mix the contents of each bowl, then cover and refrigerate for 2 hours.

CHICKEN MARINADE

1 tablespoon oyster sauce

1 tablespoon shao hsing wine

1 teaspoon light soy sauce

dash of sesame oil

To prepare the bamboo, cut the horn-shaped shoot in half lengthways, strip off the outer fibrous layers and then trim about 2 cm (1 in) off the base. Cut into 5 mm (¼ in) wide strips, add to a pan of cold salted water and then boil rapidly for at least 10 minutes. Drain and refresh under cold water. Repeat this process of boiling from a cold-water start, draining and refreshing twice more to remove any bitterness. Set aside. (Any leftover bamboo can be placed in cold water and stored in the refrigerator for up to 3 days – it makes a delicious addition to stir-fries and braises.)

BEEF MARINADE

2 tablespoons Chinese BBQ sauce

1 tablespoon shao hsing wine

1 teaspoon Sichuan pepper and salt (page 194)

dash of sesame oil

FISH MARINADE

2 tablespoons finely sliced coriander stalks and roots

1 tablespoon peanut oil

2 teaspoons sea salt

1 teaspoon white sugar

PRAWN MARINADE

1 tablespoon finely diced lemongrass

¼ cup finely sliced spring onions (scallions)

1½ tablespoons ginger julienne

1 tablespoon shao hsing wine

1 teaspoon sea salt

dash of sesame oil

1 fresh bamboo shoot – about 750 g (1½ lb)

Scrub, debeard, rinse and drain the mussels; set aside.

Clean the scallops, leaving them attached to their shells.

Trim ends from the choy sum, then cut crossways into 3 pieces and wash thoroughly; drain. Wash the asparagus and snap off the woody ends, then peel the lower part of the stem and cut into thirds on the diagonal. Discard outer leaves of cabbage, then slice cabbage in half lengthways, remove core and cut crossways into about 4 pieces and wash thoroughly, pulling pieces apart to separate leaves. Wash bean sprouts and all the herbs thoroughly; drain well. Pick sprigs from the herbs.

Blanch Hokkien noodles in boiling salted water until 'al dente' – about 4 minutes. Drain, refresh in cold water, then thoroughly drain again.

Bring a pan of water to the boil, add salted duck eggs and boil for 9 minutes. Drain, refresh in cold water, then peel and cut into quarters.

Arrange bamboo, mussels, scallops, choy sum, asparagus, cabbage, bean sprouts, herbs, noodles, eggs and mushrooms in simple serving bowls. Place these on the table, along with the bowls of marinated meats and seafood.

18 live mussels – about 350 g (11 oz) in total

12 live sea scallops

1 bunch choy sum

1 bunch green asparagus

1 Chinese white cabbage

2 cups bean sprouts

⅓ bunch mint

⅓ bunch sweet Thai basil

⅓ bunch coriander

⅓ bunch Vietnamese mint

300 g (10 oz) fresh Hokkien noodles

2 salted duck eggs

¾ cup fresh black cloud ear fungus

75 g (2½ oz) fresh shiitake mushrooms, stems discarded

6 'braised dried chinese mushrooms' (page 186)

3 litres (3 quarts) water

4 spring onions (scallions), trimmed
and cut in half crossways

10 garlic cloves, crushed

20 slices ginger

60 g (2 oz) galangal, peeled and sliced

3 lemongrass stalks, bruised

2 tablespoons sea salt

DIPPING SAUCES

combine 3 tablespoons oyster sauce
with 1 teaspoon sesame oil

combine 2 tablespoons of each of hoisin
sauce, Chinese black vinegar and Chinese
BBQ sauce

combine equal quantities of finely sliced
salted radish and pickled mustard greens

combine 1 teaspoon dark soy sauce with
2 teaspoons light soy sauce, 1 teaspoon
diced ginger and a dash of sesame oil

CONDIMENTS

light soy sauce

fish sauce

Chinese mixed pickles

finely sliced large red chillies

lemon wedges

Sichuan pepper and salt (page 194)

About an hour before your guests are due to arrive, make the stock. Place the water in a large electric wok – about 35 cm (14 in) in diameter. Add all remaining stock ingredients and bring to the boil, simmer, uncovered, for 20 minutes. Turn off heat, cover and set aside.

Finally, arrange all the dipping sauces and condiments in small bowls on the table, allowing two bowls of each.

When everyone is ready to sit down and eat, place the electric wok in the centre of the table. Reheat stock and invite your guests to choose their own meat, fish and vegetables to cook in the simmering stock, before dipping them in their favourite sauces and condiments. Towards the end of the meal – generally a long and raucous affair – the noodles are added to the rich, full-flavoured stock and slurped . . .

Enjoy!

ingredients

These are the ingredients, stocks and pickles that give my food its distinctive flavours and textures, and that I just couldn't do without!

black cloud ear fungus

Excellent eaten raw or lightly cooked, fresh black cloud ear fungus has a beautiful, velvety-smooth texture. You should be able to find fresh black cloud ear fungus (also called tree ears or wood ears) in most Asian grocers and some supermarkets. If it is unavailable, substitute with finely sliced cucumber for a similar fresh taste and slightly crunchy texture.

braised dried chinese mushrooms

These richly flavoured mushrooms keep well in the refrigerator and are perfect added to stir-fries or braises.

> 1 cup dried Chinese (shiitake) mushrooms
> ¼ cup roughly chopped ginger
> 2 spring onion (scallion) stems, halved
> 3 garlic cloves, crushed
> 2 tablespoons shao hsing wine

Soak mushrooms in hot water for 1 hour, ensuring that they are completely submerged. When softened, remove stems with scissors and discard. Place mushrooms in a pan and add enough water to cover. Add ginger, spring onions, garlic and wine, bring to the boil. Reduce heat and simmer for 45 minutes. The mushrooms are cooked when soft and tender. Allow to cool in cooking liquid.

cassia bark

The thick curls of Chinese cassia are highly aromatic, with an intense flavour that I just love, but cinnamon quills are an adequate substitute. Cassia adds a robust taste to braised dishes.

chardonnay vinegar

Chardonnay vinegar is made from chardonnay wine aged in oak barrels, and has a lovely bitter-sweet flavour. It is available at selected delicatessens, but if you can't find it, any good-quality white wine vinegar will do.

chicken stock

This is a good all-round chicken stock with clean flavours.

1 x 1.5 kg (3 lb) free-range chicken
4 litres (4 quarts) cold water
5 salad onions, trimmed and sliced
1 medium-sized leek, washed and sliced
1 medium-sized carrot, peeled and sliced
2 small sticks of celery, sliced
8 bay leaves
¼ bunch flat-leaf parsley, roughly chopped
1 garlic bulb, halved crossways
1 tablespoon white peppercorns
1 tablespoon sea salt

Rinse chicken and trim away excess fat from inside and outside cavity. Cut chicken into pieces and place in a large stockpot, along with all remaining ingredients. Bring to the boil, then reduce heat to a gentle simmer, skimming with a ladle to remove any impurities. Turn down the heat until the surface of the stock is barely moving and cook for 2 hours, skimming as required. Remove stock from stove, strain through muslin and store in refrigerator for up to 3 days, or in freezer for 2–3 months.
Makes about 3 litres (3 quarts)

chillies

The Chinese tend to prefer milder chillies, but your choice of chillies really comes down to personal taste. Small red bird's eye chillies give dishes a bite but are not as fiercely hot as some of those used in Southeast Asian cooking. Large red chillies have a slightly sweet flavour, with low to medium heat.

chinese BBQ sauce

This sticky, caramelly sauce made from soy beans, salt, sugar, garlic, pepper and Chinese five spice is perfect for marinating meats.

chinese black vinegar

This deep, dark vinegar has a complex, smoky, malty flavour that works well in stir-fries, braises and marinades.

chinese mixed pickles

Available at Asian grocers, these consist of carrots, cucumber, papaya, ginger, baby garlic cloves and other vegetables salted and then pickled in a rich, sweet syrup. They are used to enliven stir-fries and salads or as an accompaniment.
See also goong goong's pickles

choy sum

The narrow, light-green stems and darker-green oval leaves of choy sum have a delicious fresh flavour and texture. Choy sum is available in bunches from Asian grocers and most supermarkets.

cider vinegar

This is a smooth, refined vinegar with low acidity; the best has a distinct apple flavour.

dark soy sauce

This is aged for much longer than light soy sauce – and molasses is added toward the end of the processing, making it almost black in colour. Its sweeter, saltier, maltier flavour is good in braises, marinades and stir-fries. Dark soy sauce is also good as a dipping sauce.

dried sour cherries

Sold loose or in small packets at selected delicatessens and some supermarkets, these cherries have a lovely sour flavour and chewy texture.

duck eggs

I just love the rich flavour and colour of duck eggs. Fresh duck eggs are generally available from good delicatessens. If you can't find them, hen eggs are fine – just remember that they tend to be smaller, and so will need less cooking time.

enoki mushrooms

These slender-stemmed mushrooms have small, rounded caps that vary in colour from white to pale gold. In the wild, they grow on stumps of the Chinese hackberry or enoki tree, from which they take them their name. Sometimes referred to as golden needle mushrooms, their flavour is rich and yeasty. They are sold in selected greengrocers and at leading supermarkets.

fish sauce

This clear, amber-coloured liquid is the product of salted and fermented fish, and is rich in protein. Its pungently salty taste and unique, penetrating aroma are irreplaceable in stir-fries, marinades, braises, dressings and dipping sauces.

galangal

This rhizome has a slightly medicinal taste and a delicious candy-like aroma. It is used extensively in Thai cuisine and is available in Asian grocers and, increasingly, in larger supermarkets. It looks rather like ginger, but tends to be more gnarled and knobbly, with distinctive pink shoots.

garlic chives

These are the flowering stalks of the garlic plant. They have a lovely, subtle garlicky-oniony flavour, and are sold in bunches at all Asian grocers and some supermarkets.

goong goong's pickles

This recipe for homemade pickles came from my mother's father, or Goong Goong, who took great pride in growing his own vegetables and feeding his family. These pickles are delicious as a side dish, or to add piquancy to stir-fries and braises.

700 g (1 lb 6 oz) savoy cabbage

2 carrots, peeled

1 cucumber, unpeeled

1 daikon radish (mooli), peeled

1 bunch red radishes

¼ cup sea salt

2¼ cups white sugar

6 cups white vinegar

1 teaspoon chilli oil

¼ cup light soy sauce

Slice cabbage in half lengthways, remove core and cut into irregular pieces about 5 x 2 cm (2 x 1 in); roughly pull pieces apart to separate leaves. Slice cucumber and carrots in half lengthways, then cut into batons about 5 x 1 cm (2 x ½ in). Slice daikon radish in half lengthways, then cut into pieces roughly 3 x 2 cm (1½ x 1 in). Cut red radishes in half. Place prepared vegetables in a large bowl, sprinkle with salt, and mix well to combine. Cover bowl tightly with plastic wrap and refrigerate overnight. Combine sugar and vinegar in a heavy-based pan. Stir over medium heat until sugar dissolves. Simmer, without stirring, until reduced and slightly syrupy. Set aside to cool.

Next day, pour the cooled syrup over the salted vegetables. Add chilli oil and soy sauce, and mix thoroughly. Store in an airtight container in the refrigerator for 3 days to allow the flavours to develop before using. The pickles will keep, refrigerated, for several months.

Makes 2.5 kg (5 lb) pickles

hoisin sauce

This dark purplish-brown, thick, jam-like sauce is made from fermented wheat and soy beans. Its sweet, garlicky and slightly peppery taste adds depth to marinades and stir-fries; it is also used as a dipping sauce, softened with Chinese black vinegar and sesame oil.

hokkien noodles

These thick, round noodles are enriched with eggs, and the best are made with fresh eggs in the dough, rather than egg powder or yellow food colouring.

kecap manis

This thick, rich, sweetened soy sauce is most often used to add body and flavour to marinades, stir-fries and dipping sauces.

kylie's poached chicken

This chicken is poached in a light, aromatic stock, which makes it very versatile: shred for a chicken salad, such as 'poached chicken and king prawn salad with mustard fruits, celery and lemon' (page 148), or slice finely to make the most scrumptious chicken and iceberg lettuce sandwiches.

> 6 litres (6 quarts) cold water
>
> 3 spring onions (scallions), trimmed and sliced
>
> 10 garlic cloves, crushed
>
> 1 cup sliced ginger
>
> 2 tablespoons sea salt
>
> 1 medium-sized red onion, sliced
>
> 1 tablespoon white peppercorns
>
> 6 bay leaves
>
> ½ bunch flat-leaf parsley, cut in half crossways
>
> 1 x 1.5 kg (3 lb) organic free-range chicken

Place all ingredients except chicken in a 10-litre (10-quart) stockpot and bring to the boil. Reduce heat and simmer gently for 15 minutes to allow the flavours to infuse. Meanwhile, rinse chicken under cold water. Trim away excess fat from inside and outside cavity, but keep neck, parson's nose and winglets intact. Lower chicken, breast-side down, into simmering stock, ensuring it is fully submerged. Very gently poach chicken for exactly 14 minutes, then immediately remove pot from stove and allow chicken to steep in the stock for 3 hours at room temperature to complete the cooking process. Using tongs, gently remove chicken from stock, being careful not to tear the breast skin. Place chicken on a tray to drain, and allow to cool.

lemongrass

Fresh lemongrass stalks are the palest green in colour and have a subtle lemon scent. If using in a stock, cut into lengths and then bruise or crush to release the flavour. Otherwise, use only the bulb-like 10–15 cm (4–6 in) section at the base, after trimming off the top and a layer of tough outer leaves. Slice extra finely if using fresh in a salad; for pastes, slice finely before pounding with a mortar and pestle.

light soy sauce

This is the best type of soy sauce to use for stir-frying, dressing salads, braising and seasoning soups.

maggi seasoning

This Chinese type of soy sauce, made from salt, wheat, sugar and water, has an unusual and delicious flavour that is excellent in salads, noodle dishes and stir-fries.

mushroom soy sauce

This falls somewhere between light and dark soy sauce in colour. It is naturally brewed from soy beans and mushrooms. It has a delicious smoky, delicate flavour, but is very salty and should be used cautiously.

mustard fruits

These whole candied fruits preserved in a mustard-flavoured syrup are traditionally served as a condiment with boiled meats in Italy. There are many regional variations, but the most famous version is *mostarda di cremona*, which is also produced commercially and is available at selected delicatessens.

oyster mushrooms

These cream-coloured, fan-shaped mushrooms are delicate in flavour, with a rich, velvety texture. Be sure to trim off the stems, which are often chewy and tough, before use.

oyster sauce

A vital ingredient in Cantonese cuisine, oyster sauce is made from oyster extract, sugar, salt, caramel and flour. The thick, light-brown sauce has a rich flavour and is used as a condiment as well as in cooking.

palm sugar

Palm sugar is made by boiling down the sap of palm trees. It has a creamy, rich sweetness that works beautifully in desserts, but is also widely utilised in savoury dishes to balance the saltiness of fish sauce or soy sauce, the acidity of lemons or limes, and the pungency and spiciness of chillies.

preserved lemons

These aromatic lemons preserved in salt add a distinctive taste to Middle Eastern dishes – their flavour is transformed from bitter to sour-sweet. They take about a month to mature and keep well for up to a year; if you don't want to make your own, they're available at most delicatessens and some supermarkets. Always scrape away the pulp, which is very bitter, and use only the rind.

red-braising stock

This intensely flavoured stock lends a beautiful complexity to red meat dishes.

6 litres (6 quarts) cold water

3 cups shao hsing wine

2 cups dark soy sauce

1 cup light soy sauce

2 cups yellow rock sugar

12 garlic cloves, crushed

1 cup sliced ginger

8 spring onion (scallion) stems, trimmed

1 teaspoon sesame oil

10 whole star anise

¼ cup cassia bark *or* 4 cinnamon quills

1 piece dried orange peel

Place all ingredients in a 10-litre stockpot and bring to the boil. Reduce heat and simmer gently for 20 minutes to allow the flavours to infuse. The stock is now ready for use, or can be set aside to cool and then refrigerated for up to 3 days, or frozen for 2–3 months.

Makes about 6 litres (6 quarts)

red shallots

These look similar to golden shallots, but are a pinky-red in colour. They have a sweeter, more subtle flavour that's delicious in salads where you want an onion taste that complements rather than overwhelms. Red shallots are available at all Asian food stores and some supermarkets.

red wine vinegar

I like to use a red wine vinegar that's been aged in oak barrels for a smooth, rounded flavour.

rice *see* steamed rice

rice wine vinegar

I prefer to use Japanese rice wine vinegar rather than ordinary white vinegar, as it is of higher quality.

salad onions

These look like spring onions (scallions) except that they have a pronounced bulb. They're actually immature onions, with a more mellow flavour than regular onions.

salted black beans

Also known as fermented black beans, these small soy beans are preserved by fermentation with salt and spices, which gives them their distinctive, salty, rich taste and smell. There is no need to rinse them before use.

salted capers

Available in delicatessens, these have an incredibly intense and salty flavour, and so should only be used in small amounts. Always rinse off excess salt and drain before using.

sesame oil

An aromatic, strongly flavoured, nutty, golden-brown oil, sesame oil invigorates other flavours. It is generally used in small quantities so as not to overwhelm the subtleties of a dish.

shao hsing wine

Made from glutinous rice, yeast and water, this Chinese rice wine has a rich, mellow taste that enhances stir-fries and braises. It has a similar colour and bouquet to sherry – a good-quality dry sherry can be substituted if necessary.

sherry vinegar

This is made from sherry aged in oak barrels, and the best quality comes from Jerez, the sherry-producing region of Spain. It has a full, robust and rounded taste – I love the way it gives rich dishes a 'lift', cutting through the richness and acting to balance the flavours.

shiitake mushrooms

Also known as Chinese black mushrooms or golden oak mushrooms, these earthy-smelling fungi have gold to deep-brown caps with a slight bloom and creamy gills. I love their velvety, silk-like texture and the way they absorb flavours so readily. Fresh shiitake mushrooms are widely available in selected greengrocers and leading supermarkets, while dried ones are sold in most Asian stores. The tough stalks of both fresh and dried shiitakes are generally discarded before use.
See also braised dried chinese mushrooms

shimeji mushrooms

These small mushrooms have a distinctive dimple in their concave caps, are light grey to fawn in colour and have a delicate texture and flavour. They're available in selected greengrocers and leading supermarkets.

sichuan pepper

Sichuan peppercorns are reddish-brown in colour, with a strong, pungent aroma and a sharp, tingling and mildly spicy taste. They should always be dry-roasted to bring out their full flavour. For Sichuan pepper, grind with a mortar and pestle or spice grinder.

sichuan pepper and salt

I use this extensively – to season stir-fries and salads, or as an ingredient in dressings and marinades.

> 1 tablespoon Sichuan peppercorns
>
> 3 tablespoons sea salt

Dry-roast peppercorns and salt in a heavy-based pan. When the peppercorns begin to 'pop' and become aromatic, take off the heat. Allow to cool, then grind to a powder with a mortar and pestle or spice grinder.

Makes 4 tablespoons

soy sauce

This essential Chinese ingredient is made by combining soy beans, flour and water, then allowing them to naturally ferment and age for some months.
See also dark soy sauce, kecap manis, light soy sauce, mushroom soy sauce

spring onions

These unassuming green onions go under a perplexing variety of names, including scallions and green shallots. For the sake of clarity, I've called the uniformly skinny ones spring onions (scallions) in this book, while the similar-looking immature onions with a more pronounced bulb I've called salad onions.

star anise

The hard, star-shaped seedpod of the anise bush is mostly used in braises and sauces. It has an extremely robust, liquorice-like flavour and scent.

steamed rice

This is my method for perfect, fluffy white rice every time.

> 2 cups jasmine rice
>
> 3 cups water

Wash rice three times under cold running water. Strain through a colander, then put rice in a pan with a tight-fitting lid and add the water. Cover with a lid and bring to the boil. As soon as the rice begins to boil, reduce the heat to the lowest-possible setting. Cook for 12–15 minutes, leaving the lid on. Stir once with a spoon halfway through the cooking time.

Serves 4

sweet thai basil

This herb has small green leaves, purple stems and flowers, and a distinct aniseed scent and flavour. It is used in salads as an aromatic, tossed into stir-fries or curries just before serving, and as a garnish for Asian soups.

turmeric

Fresh turmeric looks like a smaller, orange-hued and less bulbous version of ginger. It should be peeled before use, but needs to be handled with care – it stains everything it comes into contact with, including hands! Fresh turmeric is becoming increasingly available in Asian supermarkets, but if you can't find it, substitute 1 tablespoon of turmeric powder for every 30 g (1 oz) of fresh turmeric required.

vietnamese mint

As its name suggests, this herb is used mainly in Vietnamese cooking – especially to add zest to chicken salads. The long, green, pointy-tipped leaves have a spicy-peppery, zingy, fresh aroma and flavour.

vinegar *see* chardonnay vinegar, Chinese black vinegar, cider vinegar, red wine vinegar, rice wine vinegar, sherry vinegar

white-poaching stock

This delicate, aromatic stock is perfect for cooking chicken and other poultry.

> 3 litres (3 quarts) cold water
> 3 salad onions, trimmed and sliced
> 8 garlic cloves, crushed
> ¾ cup sliced ginger
> 2 tablespoons sea salt
> 1 small red onion, sliced
> 1 tablespoon white peppercorns
> ½ bunch flat-leaf parsley, cut in half crossways
> 6 bay leaves

Place all ingredients in a 5-litre (5-quart) stockpot and bring to the boil. Reduce heat and simmer gently for 15 minutes to allow flavours to infuse. The stock is now ready for use, or can be set aside to cool and then refrigerated for up to 3 days, or frozen for 2–3 months.
Makes about 3 litres (3 quarts)

yellow rock sugar

Available in Asian supermarkets, this sugar tastes both richer and subtler than refined, granulated sugar. It is used mainly for braises and sauces, as it also gives them a beautiful lustre and glaze.

bibliography

Alexander, Stephanie, *Stephanie's Seasons*, Allen & Unwin, Sydney, 1993.

Alexander, Stephanie, *A Shared Table*, Viking, Melbourne, 1999.

Alexander, Stephanie, *Cooking and Travelling in South-West France*, Viking, Melbourne, 2002.

Alexander, Stephanie, and Beer, Maggie, *Stephanie Alexander and Maggie Beer's Tuscan Cookbook*, Viking, Melbourne, 1998.

Batali, Mario, *The Babbo Cookbook*, Clarkson Potter, New York, 2002.

Beer, Maggie, *Maggie's Orchard*, Viking, Melbourne, 1997.

Beer, Maggie, *Maggie's Table*, Viking, Melbourne, 2001.

Bertolli, Paul, with Waters, Alice, *Chez Panisse Cooking*, Random House, New York, 1988.

Colicchio, Tom, *Think Like a Chef*, Clarkson Potter, New York, 2000.

Cost, Bruce, *Asian Ingredients*, HarperCollins, New York, 2000.

David, Elizabeth, *An Omelette and a Glass of Wine*, Penguin, London, 1990.

David, Elizabeth, *Is There a Nutmeg in the House?*, Penguin, London, 2001.

Freson, Robert, *A Taste of France*, Stewart, Tabori & Chang, New York, 1983.

Freson, Robert, *Savouring Italy*, Pavilion, London, 1992.

Hazan, Marcella, *The Essentials of Classic Italian Cooking*, Macmillan, London, 1992.

Keller, Thomas, *The French Laundry Cookbook*, Artisan, A Division of Workman Publishing Inc., New York, 1999.

Kwong, Kylie, *Kylie Kwong: Recipes and Stories*, Viking, Melbourne, 2003.

Manfredi, Stefano, and Newton, John, *Bel Mondo: Beautiful World*, Hodder Headline, Sydney, 2000.

Norman, Jill (ed.), *South Wind through the Kitchen: The Best of Elizabeth David*, Penguin, London, 1998.

Robuchon, Joel, *Cuisines des Quatres Saisons*, Pavilion, London, 1994.

Roden, Claudia, *Tamarind and Saffron: Favourite Recipes from the Middle East*, Viking, London, 1999.

Roux, Albert and Michel, *At Home with the Roux Brothers*, BBC Books, London, 1988.

Salaman, Rena, *Greek Food: An Affectionate Celebration of Traditional Recipes*, fully revised edition, HarperCollins, London, 1993; originally published by Fontana, 1983.

Thompson, David, *Thai Food*, Viking, Melbourne, 2002.

Waters, Alice, *Chez Panisse Fruit*, HarperCollins, New York, 2002.

Waters, Alice, *Chez Panisse Café Cookbook*, HarperCollins, New York, 1999.

Wells, Patricia, *L'Atelier of Joel Robuchon: The Artistry of a Master Chef and His Protégés*, John Wiley & Sons, 1997.

Yearsley, G. K., Last, P. R. and Ward, R. D. (eds), *Australian Seafood Handbook: Domestic Species*, Fisheries Research & Development Corporation/CSIRO, Melbourne, 2001.

Yearsley, G. K., Last, P. R. and Ward, R. D. (eds), *Australian Seafood Handbook: Imported Species*, Fisheries Research & Development Corporation/CSIRO, Melbourne, 2003.

acknowledgements

Once again I have had the pleasure of working alongside the very talented and dynamic Penguin team. One of the most wonderful traits about my publisher, Julie Gibbs, is her ability to encourage and inspire. She gives you time and space to 'turn around in your basket', to contemplate exactly what it is that makes you tick, and then enables you to express it all. To Alison Cowan, my editor, you are truly gorgeous, so patient, intuitive and supportive; to designer Louise Leffler, you've done it again, blessing this book with your soulful and creative spirit; to Lindy Leonhardt, thank you for organising me, and for your strength and caring; to Bob Sessions, thank you for understanding – you have no idea how nurtured and inspired I feel when I am around you; and to Carmen De La Rue, for waving your magical production wand and making it all happen.

To Ian Wallace, for truly extraordinary photography – your skill has allowed the integrity and natural beauty of the food to leap out. To Louise Pickford, for your exquisite sense of style. To Hamish Ingham, for your inner beauty and the wonderful way you handle food – your food styling is outstanding, and you are so much a part of this book. To Simon Griffiths, another amazing photographer, I loved working with you on the set, and I just adore your sweet giggle! For beautiful props, thank you to All Hand Made, Antique General Store, The Art of Food and Wine, Bisanna Tiles, Boxx, Camargue, Cambodia House, Ici et La, Lotus Living, Made in Japan, Major and Tom, Mark Conway, Mrs Red & Sons, Off Centre, Origin Homewares, Orson & Blake, Planet Furniture, Russian Empire Trading Company, Salt Box, Tolle & Crowe and Tres Fabou.

To Jodie Tilse, for your stunningly written recipes – we make a great team! To Julz Beresford, thank you for caring so much; and to Griffith Pamment, for your beautiful cooking, but mostly for just being there – I always know that things will be okay when you're around.

With heartfelt thanks to my mother, Pauline; my father, Maurice; my brothers, Paul and Jamie; my sister-in-law, Ingrid; and to the three beautiful babies, Indy, Jyesy and Fin. You all make me so happy and fulfilled.

With deepest thanks and gratitude to Fran Moore – you are the most loyal friend anyone could ever hope to have, and your sensitivity, experience and wisdom always make me feel totally looked after. To Georgie Denier, for your support in all things and your enthusiasm; to Narelle Kellahan, for your excellent ideas, advice and friendship – I really love the way your mind works! Warmest thanks to Ervin and Charlotte Vidor, for incredible support and understanding. And the sweetest thank you to Virginia Rowlands, for sensitivity and a helping hand during this project.

With very special acknowledgements to Simon Target, my director, and the entire ABC TV crew, for taking me on and supporting me through a completely wild, wonderful, challenging and eye-opening journey! And with deepest gratitude and appreciation to all the inspiring people who allowed us into their lives and places of work.

Finally, my greatest thanks go to the team at billy kwong, led by Hamish Ingham, Danielle Renwick and Lisa Solomon. Your big hearts and creative souls make the restaurant the magical place that it is.

index

LANTERN/ABC Books

Published jointly by the Penguin Group and ABC Books for the AUSTRALIAN BROADCASTING CORPORATION

Penguin Group (Australia)
250 Camberwell Road, Camberwell,
Victoria 3124, Australia
(a division of Pearson Australia Group Pty Ltd)
Penguin Group (USA) Inc.
375 Hudson Street, New York, New York 10014, USA
Penguin Group (Canada)
90 Eglinton Avenue East, Suite 700, Toronto ON M4P 2Y3, Canada
(a division of Pearson Penguin Canada Inc.)
Penguin Books Ltd
80 Strand, London WC2R 0RL, England
Penguin Ireland
25 St Stephen's Green, Dublin 2, Ireland
(a division of Penguin Books Ltd)
Penguin Books India Pvt Ltd
11 Community Centre, Panchsheel Park, New Delhi – 110 017, India
Penguin Group (NZ)
67 Apollo Drive, Rosedale, North Shore 0632, New Zealand
(a division of Pearson New Zealand Ltd)
Penguin Books (South Africa) (Pty) Ltd
24 Sturdee Avenue, Rosebank, Johannesburg 2196, South Africa

ABC Books
GPO Box 9994, Sydney
New South Wales 2001, Australia

Penguin Books Ltd, Registered Offices: 80 Strand, London WC2R 0RL, England

First published by Penguin Books Australia Ltd and ABC Books 2003
This paperback edition published by Penguin Group (Australia)
and ABC Books 2006

10 9 8 7 6 5 4 3 2

Text copyright © Kylie Kwong 2003
Photography copyright © Ian Wallace and Simon Griffiths 2003

The moral right of the author has been asserted

All rights reserved. Without limiting the rights under copyright reserved above, no part of this publication may be reproduced, stored in or introduced into a retrieval system, or transmitted, in any form or by any means (electronic, mechanical, photocopying, recording or otherwise), without the prior written permission of both the copyright owner and the above publisher of this book.

Cover design by Patrick Leong © Penguin Group (Australia)
Text design by Louise Leffler © Penguin Group (Australia)
Photographs on cover, endpapers and pp. i, 2, 4, 8, 28, 30, 54, 78, 100, 102, 104, 124, 130, 152, 154, 178, 188 (below) and 194 by Simon Griffiths; all other photographs by Ian Wallace
The photographs on the endpapers feature Florence Broadhurst's 'Cranes' with the exclusive permission of Signature Prints Investments Pty Ltd being the exclusive licensee of the copyright in that work
Props styling by Louise Pickford
Food preparation and styling by Hamish Ingham
Typeset in Garamond by Post Pre-press Group, Brisbane, Queensland
Colour reproduction by Splitting Image, Clayton, Victoria
Printed and bound in Singapore by Imago

National Library of Australia
Cataloguing-in-Publication data:

Kwong, Kylie.
        Kylie Kwong : heart and soul.

        Includes index.
        ISBN 978 1 920989 22 4.

        1. Cookery, International. I. Griffiths, Simon.
        II. Wallace, Ian, 1959– . III. Title.

641.59

penguin.com.au